a 40-day exploration of God's goodness

what if...

LYN PACKER

What if...
Lyn Packer

Copyright © 2020 Lyn Packer

ISBN Numbers
978-0-473-55344-9 Softcover
978-0-473-55345-6 Kindle

All rights reserved. This book was published by Lyn Packer, New Zealand, under Rob and Lyn Packer Ministries. No part of this book may be reproduced in any form, by any means, without the express permission of the author. This includes reprints, photocopying, recording, or any future means of reproducing text.

If you would like to use any part of this book in articles, teachings, or any other means of recording or media, you must seek permission first by contacting me at office@robandlyn.org

Website – www.robandlyn.org

All Scriptures unless otherwise noted are taken from the NIV or the King James Version. NIV - Scripture quotations are taken from the Holy Bible, New International Version®, NIV®. Copyright © 1973, 1978, 1984, 2011 by Biblica, Inc.™ Used by permission of Zondervan. All rights reserved worldwide. www.zondervan.com
The "NIV" and "New International Version" are trademarks registered in the United States Patent and Trademark Office by Biblica, Inc.™

6	Endorsements
8	Introduction
13	1 - What If...Life with God Really is a Grand Adventure
17	2 - What If...Life in All its Fullness Really Meant a Better Life
21	3 - What If...You Can't Be Separated from the Love of God
25	4 - What If...God Is For You
29	5 - What If...God Didn't Actually Forsake Jesus on the Cross
34	6 - What If...God Really Will Never Leave Us or Forsake Us
38	7 - What If... It Actually is for Freedom that Christ Set You Free
42	8 - What If...Today You Choose Grace Instead of Perfection
47	9 - What If...I Don't Produce Enough Fruit
53	10 - What If...Old Things Really Have Passed Away
58	11 - What If...You Have Already Been Made Holy and Righteous
62	12 - What If...There Really is No Condemnation in Christ Jesus
67	13 - What If...We Really Are Blessed With Every Spiritual Blessing
72	14 - What If ...You Are a Pearl of Great Price
76	15 - What If...You Are Highly Favoured
80	16 - What If...You Are Loved, the Apple of His Eye
84	17 - What If...You Spoke to Yourself as Someone Who is Loved by God
88	18 - What If...We Lived From Delight
93	19 - What If...You Are the Habitation of God

97	20 - What If...God Has More Good in Store for You Than You Can Imagine
101	21 - What If...God Does Have a Strategy for Your Present Circumstances
105	22 - What If...In God, All Things Really Do Work Together for Good
110	23 - What If...Our Disillusionments In Life are Doing an Essential Work in Us
114	24 - What If...Everything Happening was Happening For You, Not To You
118	25 - What If...The Way God Answers our Prayers Really is for Our Good
123	26 - What If...He Who Began a Good Work in You Really Will Complete It
127	27 - What If... We Stopped Speaking the Language of Separation from God
132	28 - What If...You Have Been Created to Reign in Life
136	29 - What If...We Lived as Though We Have the Mind Of Christ
140	30 - What If...We Have Become Partakers of the Divine Nature
144	31 - What If...You Really Can Do All Things Through Christ
148	32 - What If...The Peace of God Ruled and was Guard Over my Heart
152	33 - What If...God's Plan is for the Restoration of All Things
156	34 - What If...You are Anointed and Walk in Resurrection Power
160	35 - What If...Today is a New Day Filled with Possibilities
165	36 - What If...You Carry the Same Weight of Glory that Jesus Does
170	37 - What If...Strength Sometimes Looks Different from What We've Thought
175	38 - What If...We Loved and Accepted People like Jesus Does

179	39 - What If...The Truth is Better and More Freeing Than We've Believed
183	40 - What If...We Kept Asking Questions Of What We Believe
187	Author's Bio

Endorsements

This book started as a series of devotions on Facebook, released over a forty-day period. During that time many readers asked for it to be turned into a book so they could revisit the truths again. Here's what some of the readers had to say about the series.

"I was sharing with a friend today how I don't usually like to ask questions because people will think I am stupid. Because of your posts God has given me the courage to ask them now." – Lorri.

"I'm so loving these 'what if's. Especially this one about not being able to be separated from the love of God. I so often feel like I've got to live a better life, do more good, pray more, flagellate myself for sins I've committed…. But nothing can separate us from His love!! Twisted understanding made straight. Thank you Papa!" – Jacqui.

"I love these challenges, they are getting me to check stuff out for myself. You're shining the light on Scriptures from a different direction and that is really helping me grow closer yet to our Father God. I love that as we grow in our walk with God He reveals more of Himself and His truth. It's like a kaleidoscope which is full of beautiful patterns which you see differently every time you turn it; blurry for a little while, then it clears and you see it in a different light and perspective. God reveals more truth as we learn and allow Him to reveal more of Himself each time we look at a verse and re-read it." – Lorraine D.

"Thank you for these posts. I have looked forward to each day. They challenged me, but mostly encouraged me and heartened me in my faith. This has taken me deeper into the love of the Father, and the sacrifice of Christ has much more meaning and truth to me now." – Jacquetta.

"Mic drop, truth bomb!" – Rob R.

"You certainly have a lovely way of flipping me upside down and turning me inside out. I love it!" – Lorraine R.

"Thank you, Lyn. I love the very real, honest way you write. The last few years as I have let God shake me to the core, including my theology, it's been scary, but very freeing. God bless you." – Rachael.

"Wow, I was just reading that all the fullness of God dwells in Christ, and I am now complete because of my union with Christ (Col 2:9) Awesome stuff, Lyn. This is powerful life changing revelation we all need to get a hold of!" – Cathy.

"Ngã mihi Lyn, my kuia always said things shared were pounamu and this has been such a taonga of journey with you – in all we are in Him and all He is for us. Thank you for your realness, your courage and for being the wãhine toa of the Most High that you are." – Livi.

"Clapping. Stands up. Yes, Lyn yes!" – Carina.

"Woah!! This is so good, yes! I want to hear so much more. Thank you, this so needs to be a book!!" – Paula.

"Another truth which gives me the shivers, that turns things around and reveals truth. I've never thought of that passage in that way. So, so good! Asking questions with God involved will lead to truth and freedom." – Steve.

"Thank you, Lyn, for bringing truth to the conversation, as you mentor the reader through some challenging thoughts. I love these conversations with their ability to challenge our status quo and the why and what foundations we form our thoughts and actions on. Love it!" – Petrina.

"Becoming aware of His delight in us. Love it!" – Rob L.

"Loving this frank, honest and challenging series, thank you! I need another cup of tea and more time pondering." – Janet.

"The post about striving for perfection struck such a chord in my heart, I was ushered into prayer. In His presence, listening, yearning and being surrounded by His ocean of love and grace. Yes, to the book!!" – Cynthia.

"I have deeply appreciated each of the "what if" posts over these past forty days. What a gift you've left us with. Keep asking the 'what if's Lyn." – Hana.

"That's the good news! So wonderfully explained Lyn!!!" – Helen.

Introduction

This book is a deep-dive into the goodness of the God the Father, Jesus, and Holy Spirit, and the New Covenant they made with mankind through Jesus' work on the cross. The content and subsequent writing of the book was prompted by questions I had about the things I had been taught and believed as a Christian, and the things I discovered and learnt as I explored those questions. Truth is often only discovered through asking questions, and when that discovery happens it becomes truth that we own for ourselves, not just truth that we've heard from someone else.

It's amazing how we gather ideas as we go through life. Those gathered ideas either get discarded because they're something we consider unnecessary information, or false information (a lie), or they get reinforced and filed away in our minds. Ideas that get reinforced over time become beliefs, and beliefs form our world view – they become the foundation for our core values, the way we think, the things we do, and they end up dictating how we live our lives.

Our Christian beliefs can also be formed by bits and pieces of information picked up from here and there. If we don't weigh them, check if they're true, and decide whether to keep or discard them, they get filed away in our minds as facts. Unfortunately, what we sometimes don't realise is that our mind just files them all in the 'true' file deep down in our subconscious mind. Our subconscious mind doesn't differentiate easily between true and false; it accepts all those pieces of information as fact, as being true, and that creates problems especially when it comes to us believing a lie, forming an ongoing belief from it, and then living out of it.

It's a big problem when it comes to the things we end up believing about God (the Trinity), how God views us, and what God expects from us etc. We can end up believing a toxic mix of fact and fiction, truth and lie, and believe it all to be true. It boggles the mind to think of the problems it creates for us when we live from a lie. Everything about our life gets affected – it sets the course we take, determines how we see God, ourselves and others. It's huge!

That's the purpose of this book. As an exploration of the goodness of God and the New Covenant, this book is about getting us to check if what we believe is the truth, or a distorted mix of truth and lie. Also it's about checking whether we truly believe what we say we believe. So often, what we say we believe, and what we actually believe, can be two different things!

God will question your beliefs

Over the years God Himself has questioned my theology, my beliefs about Him, what I believe Scripture says, and what I believe about myself as a result of believing those things. The truth is, when your theology is questioned – by God or by others – you can feel off-centre and even slightly unstable, but that unstable feeling only lasts until revelation of truth comes and sets you back on an even keel. However, questions are amazing things, they are at once both a tomb and a womb; a place of death and a place of new life. They are a tomb where things are laid to rest and a womb where new life forms and consequently bursts into our world, demanding both our attention and our care.

In His questioning my theology God has reframed how I've seen things and taught me to see them from a New Covenant perspective. He has taught me to not just blindly accept everything I hear and read. Understanding that my beliefs are what I see the world through has been major, and the questions I've asked have led to discovery after discovery.

> "Your assumptions (and beliefs) are your windows on the world. Scrub them off every once in a while, or the light won't come in."
> – Isaac Asimov

Some of those discoveries have led me to acknowledge that I'd believed a lie, and then taken me on to repentance (which means, in essence, having a change of mind, a radical turn around or change in what we believe). They have led me into freedom as the lie has been revealed and replaced with truth. Revelation of truth has brought me into living more and more in the glorious liberty of the sons and daughters of God! It's brought freedom, delight, tears and laughter, shouts of joy, wiggly dancing, and a deep inner knowing that God is actually good after all!

The quality of our life depends on the questions we ask. We can exist and live our lives at a surface level, never exploring or discovering much more than what we need in order to just get by, or we can embrace the gift of doubt and questioning, and in doing so discover the beauty contained in previously hidden treasures. When we ask questions we act like a miner, who suspects that there is gold hidden at a certain spot, and so he digs, he works to unearth and discover the treasure. Never belittle the ability to question; it's the only way you find the treasures hidden in life and the mysteries hidden in Christ.

Doubt is not bad!

Doubt is not something to be afraid of; it's not a sign of 'not enough faith'. Doubt is a doorway of discovery to deeper truth, when the 'doubt road' is travelled with God. Underneath our doubt is usually a fear we have, an assumption we've made or a lie that we've believed, and when we discover that thing then truth can come and set us free.

> *"By doubting, we are led to question, by questioning we arrive at the truth."*
> – Peter Abelard

Doubt that leads to questioning helps us sort out assumptions and lies from fact and truth. Embrace the doubt and questions, face them head-on; see them as doorways of discovery through which you and God can walk and journey together.

Some people don't believe that it's legitimate to question our faith, that we should just believe what we're taught; but that can be very dangerous. Questions are actually healthy and are in fact very necessary if we are to discover truth.

While questions may at first seem threatening, they only seem to be like that if we are not open to new possibilities and revelation – if we've become fixed in our thinking, or are scared of having to face the fact that we may have believed a lie or a twisted truth. The truth is that we all have questions, but sometimes we're afraid to ask them. Unfortunately the fears we have often prevent us from asking deeper questions, and we either struggle quietly with our questions or suppress them and try to ignore them altogether.

Questions can cause doubt about what we've held dear and what we've dedicated our lives to. They can cause us to be afraid to admit that we, or others, might possibly have got it wrong. Those thoughts can seek to destabilize us if we let them, but they can also spur us on to be a seeker of truth.

Allowing the things that we believe to be questioned requires that we put aside our ego, take a humble stance, and trust God with our life in a deeper, or different, way. Doing so requires us to choose courage over fear, childlikeness and discovery over safety, temporary discomfort over comfort, and it requires us to embrace the adventure that seeking truth will take us on.

Seek truth wholeheartedly

Seeking truth is something a person has to commit to doing wholeheartedly. We can't dare start asking questions unless we actually care about the answer and are willing to commit to being engaged in the process and response.

Asking genuine questions, with God involved in the process, will lead you to freedom and truth. The Trinity will be with you every step of the way; they will not abandon you in your doubts and questions, and they will not lead you into deception or try and destroy your faith. They are not deceivers or destroyers. Your faith may look different after you and God have been through the question process, but that's okay. If your faith is real, and your interaction with the question process is authentic and based in trusting the Trinity and working with them in that process, then any changes that truth brings will be good and freeing. Remember, it's for freedom that Christ set you free and He does not want you under any form of bondage or slavery.

We can unwittingly sometimes put our pastors and leaders in the Body of Christ in place as "experts" who know what they're talking about, and most often they do. But in acknowledging the fact that we often don't ask questions of what we believe, we must also accept that pastors and leaders often don't ask those questions either. They may not have asked the necessary questions in order to discover whether what they believe is truth or not.

The what-if questions in this book

Each of the forty devotions contained in this book looks at a belief that we have as Christians, challenging us to take a fresh look at it and ask questions in order to discover truth. The devotion then goes on to reveal a New Covenant understanding of truth that I pray will set you gloriously free. My hope is that as you read this book, you will do so prayerfully and with a questioning heart and mind. Allow yourself to actually ask "What is my belief around this – not just on a surface level, but what does my life show that I actually believe?" You can choose whether to read one chapter a day for forty days or take longer on any particular chapter you choose to – the journey is yours; and the joy of discovering new things, about yourself and about God, will be a part of that journey.

Journal your thoughts

In the paperback version of the book, at the end of each day's devotion, there is some journaling space. How you use that space is up to you. That space gives you the freedom and space to be honest, raw, authentic, and beautifully you; to go on an adventure of discovery with God that will take you deeper into His love. You may choose to record your thoughts and reactions to the day's devotional in words, drawings, with cut out and stuck in pictures, or you can start a conversation with God and record it there.

If you have the Kindle or PDF version there is no journaling space, so I suggest that you buy yourself a journal or notebook so that you too can also go on a journey of discovery with God.

LIFE WITH GOD REALLY IS A GRAND ADVENTURE

DAY ONE

We often start our Christian walk with the realisation that we have just started a really grand adventure, and we are so excited about it. Along the way the stuff of life happens and we can lose the sense of adventure, the sense of wonder, the sense of anticipation. Sadly sometimes we can settle into a ho-hum 'do-what's-expected-and-stick-to-the-routine' type of life and Christianity.

When we do that, often our days end up looking like this – we set off into the day with a list of instructions, jobs etc. based on what we expect to happen for that day. These instructions tell us where to go and what to do, and often, sadly, our inner compass, which once was aligned so sensitively to Holy Spirit's leading, gets set aside because we're fixated on getting the tasks on our list achieved.

Life is not a list to be completed or a predetermined set of instructions to be followed. It is, in reality, a grand adventure with the most amazing travelling companions – the Trinity. Each day you get to see what's around the next corner, explore different tracks, meet amazing people, and more.

Life is also not an endurance race where you grit your teeth and hope to make it to the end without fizzing out and running out of steam. Yes Paul likens it to a race in Scripture, but that analogy can only go so far before it runs into problems (excuse the pun). The only way that analogy works is to show us that we need to develop our character so that we may endure to the end, to get rid of the things that hinder us from following Christ, and to view Christ being formed in us as the prize.

Be careful that you don't use the race analogy to measure yourself against others. If you do it will pit you against others, make you see them as competitors, and say that you must do all you can to be better than them. One of the causes of Christians losing their sense of wonder and adventure, happens when our focus becomes all about achieving – in life and in ministry.

The analogy of your life as a race is not about proving yourself, seeing if you have what it takes to be a winner, a success and not a failure. That simply leads to a performance-based mind-set that determines your worth and value based on whether you succeed or lose. That sort of mind-set is all about having to perform – for God and for others. With that sort of mind-set we lose the wonder of adventuring with God, following Holy Spirit's leading, and those sudden detours in our day that lead us to people and places unexpected. We lose the wonder of not quite knowing what's around the next bend or what, and who, we'll encounter there. We settle for safe and predictable over curiosity and adventure.

If you've lost the sense that your life is a truly grand adventure with the Trinity as your life-long companions and adventure partners then ask for it to be restored. Tune in again to Holy Spirit's voice as you walk today's path – that nudge and whisper that says, "Check out what's over there; come and see!"

Here's a couple of ways to reawaken wonder and the sense of grand adventure – recall some of the adventures you've been on in the past with the Trinity. Also, make a gratitude list, or even better, keep an ongoing gratitude journal. This can lead to re-awakening wonder and thankfulness, which then builds a sense of anticipation about this fresh day and what it could hold.

JOURNAL PAGES...

LIFE IN ALL ITS FULLNESS REALLY MEANT A BETTER LIFE THAN YOU'VE EVER DREAMED OF

DAY TWO

God is good, God is love – these are foundational aspects of God's nature and character on which the promise of life in all its fullness is offered through Christ.

But sometimes we can look at life and circumstances and have to do some mental gymnastics to actually believe that what we currently have is life in all its fullness. I know I have, and still do on occasions. This verse challenges me sometimes, if I'm honest.

> "The thief comes only to steal and kill and destroy; I have come that they may have life, and have it to the full." John 10:10

So what does fullness of life look like? If we just focus on the physical realm and think that it applies to wealth, jobs, nothing going wrong, etc. then we will trivialise the work of Jesus in providing us with life in all its fullness. The word 'life' is 'Zoe' in the original Greek, which means *"the fullness of the life that is in God"* and *"life real and genuine, a life active and vigorous, devoted to God, blessed."*

Fullness means *"to have a superabundance of a thing"*, so when God is promising us fullness of life He's promising us that He is giving to us a superabundant, no-holds barred, poured out and overflowing river of the fullness of all He is, and all the life that is in Him.

So that provokes the question – what life is found in Him?

Life itself is in Him; without Him there is no life. Love, goodness, joy, peace, kindness, mercy, grace, favour, patience and self-control are in Him. In Him there is no lack – nothing broken, nothing missing. All provision, health, wisdom, salvation, deliverance, humility, and much more, are in Him. All these things are what He gives of Himself, and His life, to us. There is not one aspect of who we are as people that He does not give these to – our spirit, soul, body, our family life, our work life, our personal life etc. all is included.

Are there any areas in your life where you can't quite believe that God wants you to have His fullness of life? That area may be the next area where your mind is renewed, your understanding upgraded, your experience of God broadened, and your hope and faith expanded! Talk to Him about it; ask Him what lie you've believed about yourself, or about Him, that has stopped you being able to believe Him for life in all its fullness in that area.

JOURNAL PAGES...

YOU CAN'T BE SEPARATED FROM THE LOVE OF GOD

DAY THREE

The love of God is the crux, the central point of everything the church believes and teaches. It's the revelation of His love that truly changes everything for us as people. Not the revelation of our sin, but the revelation of His love – love that freely gives, that provides in every eventuality, including sin.

In Rom 8:38-39 we're told that nothing can separate us from God's love. *"For I am sure that neither death nor life, nor angels nor rulers, nor things present nor things to come, nor powers, nor height nor depth, nor anything else in all creation, will be able to separate us from the love of God in Christ Jesus our Lord."*

This Scripture gives us a list of things that cannot separate us from God's love. While it doesn't list every single thing that could potentially separate us from the love of our Father, it covers the stuff it misses with the inclusion of the words "anything else in all creation". God wants us to know that His love is that persevering and patient, and in doing so He makes sure everything is covered. Here it is again: there is nothing that can separate us from His love—not even ourselves.

As Christians, for the most part, we accept this verse as truth, but we don't always feel the truth of it in our lives. Many of us have lived at least some of our Christian life with a fear that skews our understanding of this verse (and others like it). We read it and think that while nothing outside can separate ourselves from His love, we can separate ourselves from it. Fear whispers to us that we may, in some way or other, do something that will separate ourselves from that love. And as that fear takes hold the devil plays with our mind and heart until we've somehow built up in our mind an indisputable, yet untrue, case for why we can be separated from God's love.

But let's unpack this verse and look at it a bit closer. This verse is talking about us as humans, and the things that we may encounter in life – death, life, things present and things to come, angels and demonic powers, earthly powers, natural disasters – it's all listed there, even if not specifically named. If nothing in creation can separate us from God's love, and we as humans are part of the creation mentioned in this verse, then even we cannot separate ourselves from His love. It's actually simple; you are in Christ and therefore can never be separated from His love. Full stop, the end!

Today know this, celebrate this, revel in it – His love for you is sure, it is eternal, it is never-changing and you can know, and live in, the security of it. Nothing you, or anything else, can do can separate you from His love. You may not always experience the feelings of His love, but feelings are not always an accurate indicator of truth. Whether you feel loved by Him today or not, the truth has not changed – you are in Christ and secure in Him; even your sin can no longer separate you.

JOURNAL PAGES...

GOD
IS FOR
YOU

DAY FOUR

Romans 8 is an epic chapter full of the rich goodness of God toward us and in the midst of it Paul makes this statement, *"If God is for us, who can be against us."* Here they were as Christians – hated, and even feared by many, persecuted by both civic and religious leaders, and in some cases even put to death. They needed this reminder that they were not facing things alone, just as we sometimes need to be reminded of it. Whatever you're facing today you don't face it alone!

Throughout the Bible we see many examples of the fact that God is for us, but for the sake of time and space I want to list some that Romans 8 alone tells us. Some of these I will just list because we cover them more fully in other chapters.

- There is now no condemnation to those in Christ Jesus (verse 1). Who can condemn you and it hold weight eternally? No-one! We may suffer earthly condemnation – people may rise up against us, but God promises even then to cause those unrighteous judgements to be refuted in the end. (See Isa 54:17.)

- He has set us free from the law of sin and death (verse 2).

- He has given us His dear Son, who willingly laid down His life for our freedom (verse 3).

- He has given us His Spirit (verse 9), dwelling in us, helping us. The following are some of the things Holy Spirit does, according to this chapter...
    1. Holy Spirit has come to indwell us (verse 9). This is true of every child of God.
    2. That indwelling is in order to give us life (verse 10). See 2 Pet 1:4.
    3. Holy Spirit's indwelling guarantees our resurrection (verses 11,23).
    4. Holy Spirit sets us free (verse 13). See verse 2.
    5. Holy Spirit is our constant guide (verse 14) and leads us according to God's will.
    6. Holy Spirit in us, gives us assurance that we really are the Lord's (verse 16).
    7. Holy Spirit indwells us to be our Helper (verse 26).

- The Father has adopted us into His family and made us His children (verse 14).

- The Father has made us joint-heirs with Christ (verse 14).

- He has promised us that all things work together for our good (verse 28).

- He has called us, justified us, and glorified us (verses 29-30).

- He has given us eternal security by promising that nothing can ever separate us from His love (verses 35-39).

There is so much in this chapter alone that could have us jumping up and down, giving thanks and making happy faces all day long as it comes back to our minds over and over. God is so good! He loves you and He is for you. He has proven it time and time again; He has proven His trustworthiness, His faithfulness, His goodness, His love, His provision. While there may be some things, or people, on earth that may rise against you, God is for you, He will come to your aid and defence, He will be your help in times of need, your strong deliverer, your refuge, and more.

JOURNAL PAGES...

GOD DIDN'T ACTUALLY FORSAKE JESUS ON THE CROSS, WHAT IF HE JOINED HIM THERE

DAY FIVE

We read in our Bibles Jesus' statement on the cross, *"My God, my God why have you forsaken me"* and we think that God turned His back on His Son. We think that sin had made Jesus so repulsive to God that He could not even bear to look on Him.

I don't know if your mind does the mental gymnastics mine does, but I used to believe that while my past sin was forgiven, because I'd asked God to forgive it, my present or future sin could still separate me from God and make Him forsake me. What if that is not true? What if we've read it wrong and even been taught wrong? I want to present another possibility from Scripture and from Jesus' own words. I want you to see that God will not turn His back on you, because He did not turn His back on Jesus.

So, back to Jesus' statement on the cross. Did God the Father turn His back on Jesus and forsake Him, or was something quite different from what the words seem to imply actually happening? My research has led me to believe that something different was happening.

Why? Throughout His lifetime Jesus made some interesting claims...

Let's start with His claims about the oneness between Him and the Father – *"I and my Father are one."* John 10:30. And in John 14:9-11 Jesus says four times that He and the Father are in each other. That reality was never rescinded – before, during, or after the cross.

In speaking of His coming death, Jesus firmly believed, and stated, that the Father would not leave Him to face it alone.

"So Jesus said, *"When you have lifted up the Son of Man, then you will know that I am he and that I do nothing on my own but speak just what the Father has taught me. The one who sent me is with me; he has not left me alone, for I always do what pleases him."* John 8:28,29.

"A time is coming and in fact has come when you will be scattered, each to your own home. You will leave me all alone. Yet I am not alone, for my Father is with me." John 16:32.

Then we come to those famous words on the cross... *"My God, my God why have you forsaken me."* (Matt 27:46).

Those words, *"My God, my God why have you forsaken me"* were not Jesus' personal cry; they are a quote of the first verse of Psalm 22, the prophetic, messianic psalm of deliverance written by David that begins with that cry, but goes on to say that God hasn't despised him or his cry, he has not hidden his face from him, he has heard when he cried to him, and the passage ends with the declaration, *"he has done it!"* In other words, *"It is finished"*, he has delivered us! David is telling us ahead of time that Jesus will die and yet the Father will not turn His face from Jesus on the cross.

In quoting this phrase from Psalm 22 Jesus uses a traditional Rabbinical teaching method where they used the first statement from a passage of Scripture, and through doing so, their students knew what they were referring to and where they were going to be speaking from. This statement on the cross refers those people at the cross back to that passage of deliverance in Psalms. Most of the Jews listening, especially any Pharisees or Sadducees there, would know by His statement that Jesus was referencing David and this Psalm. They knew their Scriptures and were familiar with the Messianic prophecies. For those that heard this cry in the right way, they would have heard that Jesus did not feel forsaken; they would have heard that He was proclaiming hope and deliverance, they would have heard Him reveal that He was the Messiah.

Paul reinforces the fact that God the Father did not forsake Jesus on the cross, in 2 Cor 5:19, *"...God was in Christ, reconciling the world unto himself, not imputing their trespasses unto them."*

GOD WAS IN CHRIST! They hung there as one!

The Amplified Bible says it like this, *"It was God [personally present] in Christ, reconciling and restoring the world to favour with Himself, not counting up and holding against [men] their trespasses [but cancelling them], and committing to us the message of reconciliation (of the restoration to favour)."* (AMP)

Wow, God was personally present in Christ on the cross! He did not forsake Jesus or turn His back on Him in the hour He most needed Him; He joined Him on that cross in bearing our sin. This truth has huge significance for us in our struggles, in our pain, and times of feeling isolated and abandoned, as we'll see in the next chapter.

JOURNAL PAGES...

GOD REALLY WILL NEVER LEAVE US OR FORSAKE US

DAY SIX

In the last chapter, where we talked about the reality that God the Father didn't forsake Jesus on the cross, we affirmed that the Trinity will never leave us or forsake us either. Scripture is crammed with verses that talk about that fact and I read at least twelve that explicitly said that while researching and preparing this material, and there were at least another hundred that alluded to the same reality.

As I read them I was reminded of our traditional western wedding vows where one partner promises the other "to have and to hold from this day forward, for better, for worse, for richer, for poorer, in sickness and in health, to love and to cherish, till death do us part." We have something better than a human wedding vow; we have a Covenant with the God who does not lie, the one who is Truth itself and, unlike human wedding vows, the Covenant God has made with us cannot be broken and does not end at death.

Nothing in heaven or on earth can break the Covenant that God has made with mankind. In your best times and your worst, in sickness and health, whether rich or poor, God, Jesus, and Holy Spirit will all be with you. They will be with you in everything as your constant companions, your source of strength and encouragement, your wisdom, your guides, your friends, your wise counsellors, the ones who stick closer than a brother. You will not be rejected, abandoned, or left to face things on your own. You can know security – and that's the truth.

You can trust the Trinity – they will not abandon you in the hour of your greatest need, they will not abandon you because of sin, they will not abandon you, full stop! God the Father never abandoned Jesus and He will not turn His back on you, nor abandon you either.

If you want to check for yourself some of the verses that show God promising over and over to never leave or forsake those He loves, here's a few to start with... Deut 31:6,8; Heb 13:5; Josh 1:5,9; Psa 94:14; Deut 4:31; Matt 28:20; Psa 27:10; Isa 41:17; John 14:18; 1 Kings 6:13; 1 Sam 12:22; Psa 37:28; John 14:1-31. And as I said before, there are many, many more.

JOURNAL PAGES...

IT ACTUALLY IS FOR FREEDOM THAT CHRIST SET YOU FREE

DAY SEVEN

Gal 5:1 "So Christ has truly set us free. Now make sure that you stay free, and don't get tied up again in slavery to the law."

This is a biggie – freedom from the law of Moses and the laws of the Pharisees, the laws of religion. But do we actually believe it?

The law reveals our sinfulness, but it cannot provide a way out. Until Christ came the Jews *"were held in custody under the law, locked up until the faith that was to come would be revealed. So the law was our guardian until Christ came, that we might be justified by faith."* (Gal 3:22–24).

Paul says in Romans 7:7-8 and 1Corinthians 15:56 that the law does not help you overcome sin. Rather, the law helps sin to overcome you! He writes to the early church telling them that Jesus is the only one who ever kept the law of Moses perfectly, and then He died to pay the penalty for the sins of others. Those who continue to follow the law in order to be right before God are still slaves to their own sin (Gal 4:8–9). Those who come to God by faith in Christ are free.

In Galatians 5 Paul repeats that message and adds a call to rebellion against sin and slavery. He tells the Galatians, and by extension all Christians, that Christ has set us free so we ought to stand firm. We should not take that yoke of slavery again. In other words believers ought not let anyone tell them that they must follow all of the rules and restrictions of the law of Moses to be right with God. I often hear Christians say that we should still follow the law as well as believing in Jesus and it is this very thing that Paul is addressing.

But our reality is that Christ has given us a new nature, one freed from the bondage of sin and law, a nature like His and we are growing up into maturity in that nature and bearing fruit of it in our lives. We are no longer under the reign of a sinful nature, and because of that, our desires are different now, our base nature is different; we live from a nature that is loving, kind, merciful, patient, etc.

He has freed us from the 'have-to's, 'should's and 'must's of religious law. I know that for some of you reading this you will strongly disagree; others will read it as me saying that you can go ahead and do anything you want, that you can sin as much as you like. That's not what I'm saying.

I'm saying that Christ has set you free from the law, which Scripture plainly tells us inflamed sin within us and kept us as prisoners to sin. I'm saying live from your new nature, as one freed from the constant battle to have to live under laws, expectations, of constantly battling to try and be good, to try and do right, and failing over and over. Days 10 and 11 in this book will give you a fuller understanding of this.

Can we learn some good stuff by reading about the Old Testament laws and their effect on the children of Israel? Absolutely! But those laws passed away and became obsolete with Jesus' death and resurrection (Heb 8:13). They are not the laws of the New Covenant. Under the New Covenant Jesus commands us to live from love – to love one another as Christ loved us. The answer to sin is not to live under the Old Covenant's laws, it is found in being set free to live as love! All sin violates love in some way – the sins of stealing, lying, murder, impatience, gossip, etc. – they all violate love and living a lifestyle of loving others.

Live from love and the grace Jesus has released into your life. His grace empowers us and trains us to say no to ungodliness (Tit 2:12). It actually *"equips us to live self-controlled, upright, godly lives in this present age."* (The Passion Translation)

Trying to produce the fruit of godliness in your life by your own efforts and law-keeping will only frustrate the purposes of God in your life. You'll end up being both barren and miserable. Instead, the fruit that Christ desires to bear in us will grow naturally as we abide in Him (John 15:7-9).

Rely on the law to make or keep you righteous and, as Scripture says, you'll live under a curse – *"all who rely on the law are under a curse"* (Gal 3:10). Rely instead on Christ's grace at work in your new nature and you will live a life that is holy, righteous, and loving, and you'll do it naturally because that's now who you are – you are love learning to manifest itself in this world we live in.

JOURNAL PAGES...

TODAY YOU CHOOSE GRACE INSTEAD OF PERFECTION

DAY EIGHT

I have to admit, I've struggled with performance-based acceptance issues and perfectionism over the years and I can place a lot of pressure on myself to get something just right. Of course that's caused some very real stress and feelings of not measuring up.

Imagine this if you will – I'm in my twenties, a pastor's wife with two young kids. It's the 1980's, the era of big hair, shoulder pads, Sunday best clothes for church, make-up every day, and I was expected, as a pastor's wife, to always look the part (so I found out pretty quickly). You're probably beginning to get the idea of where I'm going. Expectations plus performance-based acceptance issues and underlying perfectionism in order to prove my worth... Add to that what I felt God expected of me and there we have a perfect environment for me feeling a failure almost constantly on one level or another.

I tried so hard to fit both my own and others' expectations of what a pastor's wife should look like and act like. I wanted to do it right (read that as perfect) and it was expected that pastors' wives would look and act a certain way because, after all, we represented the church that our husbands pastored....But trying to be the perfect pastor's wife and perfect Christian left me stressed-out and frazzled.

What was the answer? What keys did I find? What steps did I take? Were there ten steps and three keys to being the perfect Christian, as so many sermons seemed to suggest? No! The answer was simple, as answers in God's Kingdom usually are. The answer was in accepting the grace of God.

Jesus offers us a life of freedom from perfectionism and religious 'should's, 'have-to's and 'must's, a life where we can walk in the unforced rhythms of His grace. He says to us *"Are you tired? Worn out? Burned out on religion? Come to me. Get away with me and you'll recover your life. I'll show you how to take a real rest. Walk with me and work with me—watch how I do it. Learn the unforced rhythms of grace. I won't lay anything heavy or ill-fitting on you. Keep company with me and you'll learn to live freely and lightly."* Matt 11: 28-30.

Paul tells us this also in 2 Cor 12:9 *"But he said to me, "My grace is sufficient for you, for my power is made perfect in weakness."*

Paul knew what it was to suffer from the tyranny of religious perfectionism. He'd been a Pharisee (Acts 23:6; 26:5; Phil 3:5). Pharisees were legalists and perfectionists in following the law to an extreme; they even strove to be perfectionists in protecting their perfectionism. In their world if you did everything the law said then you were okay, and if not you were 'out', looked down on, and considered a disappointment. It sounds a bit like what we still see and feel sometimes today, doesn't it? Then Paul had a life-changing encounter with Jesus and he went from being a perfectionist and legalist to someone who championed freedom and grace. Look at his writings; they are full of how amazing God's grace is for sinners and messed up perfectionists like himself and us.

Today that same grace is there for you and I to receive and live in. One of the most important ways we can escape the tyranny of perfectionism is to discover grace. And the cool thing about grace is you don't have to be perfect to qualify for it or embrace it. Grace is free and available to all.

But what is Grace? Grace is the manifested, love, favour, kindness and graciousness of our Creator and Father, given to us freely. It is not only able to be understood, but also to be experienced.

When we don't understand this beautiful gift we strive and try to obtain the goodness and acceptance of God. Grace tells us that we cannot do anything to earn forgiveness, become holy, or become righteous… because He has already given us these things!

Grace sets us free from the pressure of performance oriented living and empowers our growth. Paul tells us, *"the grace of God has appeared, bringing salvation for all people, training us to renounce ungodliness and worldly passions, and to live self-controlled, upright, and godly lives"* (Titus 2:11,12).

Grace transforms our desires, motivations, and behaviour, and it grounds and empowers everything in the Christian life. Living by grace doesn't mean you get to be lazy, sloppy about behaviour, sin as much as you want to, or treat others badly. Grace is what gives us the power to live as authentic sons and daughters of God who are holy and righteous. It's something that we both receive and grow in, with grace making room for growth and giving the resources we need for that growth to happen. We *"grow in the grace and knowledge of our Lord and Saviour Jesus Christ"* (2 Pet 2:18). It gives us the freedom to be our true self, freed of false expectations or having to strive under the weight of performance based acceptance.

Now, because of grace, I'm set free from the pressure of perfectionism and I'm learning to walk without the pressure of religious expectation, in the unforced rhythms of the grace gifted to me by Jesus, and I'm loving it! Come and join me. Jesus guarantees that you'll never regret ditching perfectionism, or a performance-based mentality, and trading it in for freedom and grace.

JOURNAL PAGES...

I DON'T PRODUCE ENOUGH FRUIT

DAY NINE

How much do I have to do to be a good Christian? And what happens if I'm not good enough? What if I don't produce enough fruit, don't pray enough, don't fast enough, or don't read my Bible enough? Many Christians live their whole life with these questions simmering away underneath everything. They live with pressurizing thoughts such as, "If I do pray, fast and read my Bible consistently and well that will prove I love God, and maybe He won't be angry or disappointed in me." Or "If I prove my love by being obedient, praying heaps, fasting, etc. then Jesus won't cut me off."

Thoughts like these are often based on what has turned out to be a mistranslation of some verses in Scripture. In John 15:1 Jesus talks about Himself as being the vine and us as the branches of that vine.

The NIV translates it as…"*I am the true vine, and my Father is the gardener. ² He cuts off every branch in me that bears no fruit, while every branch that does bear fruit he prunes so that it will be even more fruitful.*"

In this translation and in traditional teaching we are taught that branches that don't bear fruit are cut off from the vine and taken away to be burned. But is that a correct understanding and translation? The Greek word translated as "cut off" in this passage is *airo* and it's primary meaning is *lift up*. Here are some examples of other situations where Jesus used the same word. *"If any man would come after me, let him deny himself, and take up his cross, and follow me"* (Matt 16:24). *"They will pick up snakes with their hands; and when they drink deadly poison, it will not hurt them at all"* (Mk 16:18). *"Rise, take up thy bed and walk"* (John 5:8). In none of these verses was the word *airo* translated as "cut off", nor would it have made sense to do so, yet some translators chose to translate it as that in the passage in John 15.

Jesus often talked about the culture and farming practices of His day and in this instance He talks about growing vines and harvesting grapes. Vines were grown differently in Jesus' time from how they are today. Over recent years, with many historical documents now able to be more easily accessed, we have greater understanding of how the vine-dressers of His day looked after their grapes. The grape vines and branches weren't supported by wires and fence poles as they are today; that came centuries later. In Jesus' day branches were propped up off the ground with rocks or old branches to stop the grapes rotting on the ground, or they grew along the tops of shallow walls.

The gardener or vine-dresser regularly inspected his grape vines to make sure that there was no disease, no fruit bearing branches laying on the ground where the grapes could get ruined. Any branches that were not fruit bearing were first lifted up off the ground and supported by rocks to stop them taking root in the soil, so that they had a better chance of fruiting. By lifting them up their growth would go into producing fruit, not into growing roots (grapevines being like many other vines which grow fresh roots wherever they lay on the ground). If a branch was diseased then he would cut the diseased bits off to encourage the branch to produce fruit.

The vine-dresser would do everything in his power to bring fruitfulness to the branch, caring for it, lifting it up to the light, cutting away disease, etc. in order to help the branch produce fruit. So it is with us. The Father cares for us and will do everything in His power to help us be fruitful. To live with the pressure and underlying fear of being cut off by God for normal human frailty or a lapse in discipline is to live an intolerable life of torment based on believing that God is a God who rules by fear of punishment. That's not the loving Father that Jesus revealed to us.

Good works, attendance at things, volunteering for everything, prayer, self-denial, sin consciousness etc. can all become very performance-oriented instead of relationship-oriented. We try to live like we believe a Christian should in order to make God happy or pleased with us. We try hard to not sin, and we think our efforts can make God be more pleased with us than He is. Yet the vine branches produce fruit not by trying to prove themselves, but because the life giving flow from the vine provides them with all they need to naturally produce fruit. So it is with us. If we are connected with Christ everything we need to grow and produce fruit is provided by Him. His life-force, His essence, flows into us and works in us. His essence is His nature and character – who He is, and His life force is His power. They are both at work in us and we need not fear that it won't be enough to naturally produce fruit in our lives as we remain surrendered and connected to Him.

God cannot do more for us than He already does. We are loved and accepted by Him and are now in Christ in a state of oneness that is a wondrous mystery which, while we may not fully understand it, is still true. (John 3:16; Eph 1:6; Rom 8:35-39.)

Here's the good news about the question I asked earlier – what if I don't produce enough fruit, don't pray enough, don't fast enough, or don't read my Bible enough?

- We aren't justified (made good enough) by our works, but by His work. It's through faith in Christ's work that we are justified, made holy and righteous. (Gal 2:16.)

- We don't owe God. He didn't do what He did so that we would owe Him, and do things for Him – that would make Him a God who manipulates in order to get His way. It was a free gift. You don't owe someone who gives you a gift that is given with love. (Eph 2:8.)

- We don't have to try to keep in His good books by behaving a certain way. We are loved and accepted unconditionally as His beloved children because of what Christ did. We are accepted in the beloved. (Eph 1:6.)

- Just as we were saved by grace, so we are kept by His love and grace. Love and grace keep us, sustain us and establish us in relationship with Him and in our faith walk. (Col 2:6.)

- God the Father (the vine-dresser) will do everything in His power to give us the right conditions so that fruit bearing happens naturally in our lives – lifting us up, caring for us, pruning back old fruiting branches to enable us to produce new fruit, cutting out disease, etc. I suggest you read John 15 in the Passion Translation – it gives a far more accurate translation of these verses than older translations.

- We can't finish (in our strength) what He started. He will complete the good work started in us. He is the author and finisher of our faith (Heb 12:2), and what was begun by the Spirit cannot be perfected by the flesh. (Gal 3:3.)

Christ's work, over His lifetime and on the cross, did what we could never do in our own strength; it justified us and made us right with God, made us righteous, pure and holy. Are we encouraged to live holy, righteous lives? Yes. Are we encouraged to read the Word, to pray, to fast? Yes, and it is our great pleasure to do so. Why? Because we know that those things help us with our growth and are an expression of our loving relationship with the Lord; they are not something we have to do to stay in His good books.

JOURNAL PAGES...

OLD THINGS REALLY HAVE PASSED AWAY

DAY TEN

You probably know the verse I'm referring to in the statement above... *"If anyone is in Christ, he is a new creation. The old has passed away; behold, the new has come."* (2 Cor 5:17). In 2 Pet 1:4 we also read that we have become partakers of the divine nature.

I lived much of my earlier Christian life tormented by the seeming contradiction and challenge that these verses presented to me. If they were true then I seemed to be living a lie as a Christian. I didn't seem to be a totally different person at all, just someone who was now aware of a titanic daily struggle to be someone I thought God expected me to be, but could never actually be. I believed, and the Bible seemed to indicate, that I still had a sinful nature and would fight it for the rest of my life, until I died. Only then would I be rid of my sinful nature.

Either I was doomed to live a schizophrenic, double natured Christianity or something was wrong. If I am a new creation but still have a sinful nature as well, then two things must be true...

1. I am doomed to live a life torn between two natures that will fight within me until I die, and if that's true then what's also true is

2. natural death is my saviour – my perfecter, the bringer of wholeness – not Christ

Me being me, that realisation spurred me to research in order to discover the truth, and what I found was that a mistranslation had taken place in the version of the Bible I read, an early version of the NIV. It wasn't until I began to check it against other versions and look at my concordance and some reference books that I discovered that mistranslation.

Research showed me that I actually didn't still have a sinful nature. Many of the verses translated 'sinful nature' in the NIV were actually mistranslations; the words actually mean 'flesh, sensual nature or fleshly behaviour'. That refers to our habitual ways of responding, patterns of behaviour that we have learnt and got stuck in over the years, not who we are – not our core reality, our nature.

The things I was struggling with – the sins, the habitual ways of doing things, of thinking – were habitual patterns of behaviour that I had established over my earlier years. They were not my nature, not the true essence of who I was, my core being. And those things were changeable. Over time as I grew in my new nature, my new identity, they were becoming more and more what they actually were – fading echoes of an old life, the old me.

I had bought so deeply into the belief that I still had a sinful nature that I couldn't see that over time I had been sinning less, I had been making better choices, I had been changing habitual ways of behaviour and thinking. This was because the new me – the new creation I'd become in Christ, the whole, holy, pure, righteous creation – was working to change me from the inside out, exerting its influence over my mind and flesh, and the fruit of my new creation nature, the nature and character of Christ, was manifesting in me.

Some habit patterns didn't break off until I realised what they were and got a strategy from God for changing them; some just fell away, quietly and unnoticed, as my renewed nature and mind created new habit patterns and ways of thinking that became stronger than the old ones. Then sometimes a realisation would hit me – I was no longer doing or thinking such and such any more. I had changed, I was different.

If you are in Christ you no longer have a sinful nature; you are a new creation and your old habitual ways of thinking and behaving are but fading echoes of your old life.

You really are a new creation in Christ! Have a look back over your life. How different are you now from what you were before you came to Christ? How has your new nature been asserting itself in your life and changing things without you even realising? What a glorious revelation – you no longer have a sinful nature! That is gone and your new nature is revealing in you more and more of the nature and character of Christ. That's something to celebrate today, that's something to praise God for!

(My suggestion – don't rely on one version of the Bible alone, read different ones to get a better picture of what the original texts mean. Also make use of concordances and reference books but remember that translators are human;

they can make mistakes and sometimes bring their biases and beliefs to their translation work; they shouldn't, but they do.)

JOURNAL PAGES...

YOU HAVE ALREADY BEEN MADE HOLY AND RIGHTEOUS

DAY ELEVEN

I used to spend so much time worrying that God wouldn't see me as holy enough, despite what I felt were my best efforts at not sinning, keeping my thoughts under control, spending loads of time praying, worshipping, and reading my Bible. I used to wonder when enough would be enough and I'd cross that unseen threshold into being holy. I thought that I'd never be fully holy until I died, and that death would magically transform me into being completely pure and holy. I felt that I was condemned to live life in pursuit of holiness, with God somehow being disappointed in me because I felt I would never quite get there before I died.

I thought I'd read the Bible and understood it, but I hadn't. One day one of those revelatory lightbulb moments happened and I realised that Christ had done those things – He had made me holy and righteous before God – Scripture actually said that, but I hadn't seen it. And my part in it all was simply to learn how to walk in it.

Holiness means wholeness, and completeness, and out of that wholeness comes wholesome behaviour. Holiness is not just about us needing to have moral standards, some code of ethics we live from; it's a fundamental change to who we are. We were sinners; now we are holy and righteous in Christ. Holiness and righteousness are attributes of our new nature, gifted to us when we believed Christ. They aren't something we have to try and become, they are who we are, and we are learning to live from them.

When Jesus said be perfect/holy as your Father in heaven is perfect/holy, He was pronouncing wholeness over us and into us, not commanding us to try and become something. He was saying, "Be whole, as your Father in heaven is whole."

The Bible proclaims that...

- We were sanctified (1 Cor 6:11).

- We have been made holy through His sacrifice and perfected forever (Heb 10:10,14).

- We are complete in Christ (Col 2:10).

- We have been set free from sin and our present reward is wholeness (Rom 6:22).

- We are God's chosen people, a royal priesthood, a people belonging to God (1Pet 2:9).

- We have been called to a whole, complete life through His grace (2 Tim 1:9; 1 Cor 1:2).

- Our new self is created to be like God in true righteousness and wholeness (Eph 4:24).

We may not always feel like those things are true, but they are. You and I are holy and righteous already.

Martyn Llyod-Jones is quoted as saying, *"Holiness is not something we are called upon to do in order that we may become something; it is something we are to do because of what we already are..."*

Maybe instead of expending all our effort into trying to become good enough to please God, we could live from the holiness or wholeness Christ gave us, knowing that Christ has made us pleasing to God already, and He has given us a new holy, righteous nature. Or, as my husband Rob says sometimes, *"What would it look like if we took our holiness out for a spin and checked out how it functioned?"*

JOURNAL PAGES...

THERE REALLY IS NO CONDEMNATION FOR THOSE IN CHRIST JESUS

DAY TWELVE

"Therefore, there is now no condemnation for those who are in Christ Jesus, because through Christ Jesus the law of the Spirit who gives life has set you free from the law of sin and death." (Rom 8:1-2)

These verses should be a great comfort to Christians, but often they're not. Why? Because we still often hear the voice of accusation in our heads and think that the feeling of being accused is what this verse is talking about. However accusation is different from condemnation. Accusation is a charge or claim that someone has done something wrong. Condemnation, or being condemned, is a sentencing for punishment.

I used to think being accused was the same as being condemned. Accusation can come from several sources – our own heart and mind, other people, and the Kingdom of Darkness (Satan's realm). The accusation from these three sources usually comes with the purpose of pointing out wrong and with a purpose of making us feel shame and guilt. It says, "Guilty until proven innocent." It makes a guilty judgement before the facts are known. God never accuses us because He has no interest in making us feel dirty, shameful, etc. He may point out to us areas in our lives that need change but that is different from accusation which carries shame in it.

The words condemn and convict are legal sentencing terms – pronouncements of guilt with the purpose of giving a sentence or assigning a punishment. Because of our understanding of that meaning for those words, it makes us view verses like John 16:8 where it talks about Holy Spirit convicting the world of sin from a wrong perspective and makes us think Holy Spirit is continually pronouncing us guilty.

What we, as Christians call the conviction of Holy Spirit (John 16:8) means something different The use of the words 'convicts' on the part of the translators was a poor word choice considering the meaning of the original word which means 'rebuke, reprove, convince, convict'. Holy Spirit doesn't ever come to convict us in a sentencing way but to convince us; the Trinity's own judgement of "all sin is forgiven" shows us that. The Douay-Rheims translation gives a better translation of it – *"And when he (Holy Spirit) is come, he will convince the world of sin and of justice and of judgment."* Holy Spirit comes to convince us concerning sin, not to accuse or condemn us. As non-Christians Holy Spirit seeks to convince us that sin has dominion over us and that Jesus is offering us freedom from the tyranny we are under. As Christians Holy Spirit works to show us or convince us of where change is needed so that we live in line with our new creation nature. He knows all the facts, takes our righteousness into consideration, and calls us to live out of who we really are in Christ. And then He supplies the spiritual resources we need to walk differently – strength, joy, encouragement, courage, wisdom etc.

Maybe we just need to believe the overarching truth of this very emphatic statement of Paul's, (and the rest of Scripture), that if we are in Christ there is now no condemnation for us. Your sins are forgiven – past, present and future sins. You now live in a permanent state of having been forgiven, and you have been set free from sin's dominion. There is no threat of a sentence or penalty hanging over your life because you are in Christ. You have been made the righteousness of God in Christ (2 Cor 5:21).

Later in Romans 8, in verse 33, Paul goes on to say, *"Who shall bring any charge against God's elect? It is God who justifies."* Paul uses legal language here and in doing so he is in effect saying that no-one has the right to demand that we be condemned by God. Satan is revealed in Rev 12:10 as the accuser of the brethren and he may still try to accuse us, but his accusations no longer hold the power to even seek a sentence of condemnation; that right was stripped from him at the cross.

Sometimes, however, he will try and get us to think that he still has the right to condemn us. He does so by seeking to get us to come into agreement with him and to use our own thought life against us. He taunts us with our sin and mistakes, seeking to make us feel unworthy, and hinting that God could never forgive us of "that" and "could never love someone who does that". When we come into agreement with his accusation then we seek to try and find ways to get out from under it. We do so by buying into religious formulas and seeking keys that will unlock our prison of condemnation. But maybe instead we need to believe God's Word, stand firm, and resist the devil instead of believing him and allowing him to bring us into condemnation (James 4:7).

Paul is very clear – Satan's accusations hold no legal power any longer. Why? Not on the basis of our perfect behaviour, but because God has forgiven us and declared us righteous based on our faith in Christ's work. He has credited us with Jesus' own righteousness. So if God judges us on the basis of Jesus' righteousness how can we ever be condemned. God will never condemn Jesus so He will never condemn us. We are free from all condemnation.

That doesn't mean that we live any old how or think we can do anything and there will be no consequences. Sin has consequences. Doing dumb things has consequences and has subsequent ripple effects that can spread and cause further damage, but we need not live in fear. God has made a way in relationship for us come to Him, to repent – see from His perspective, change our thinking, and come into agreement with that in a way that causes a change in the way we live – and to move forward, free from all condemnation.

JOURNAL PAGES...

WE REALLY ARE BLESSED WITH EVERY SPIRITUAL BLESSING IN THE HEAVENLY PLACES

DAY THIRTEEN

In my family, and amongst those I grew up with, "Bless you" was something you said when someone sneezed. I had no idea what it meant, and then later I heard people say they'd been blessed when something kind was done for them, or they received something good. Or if I did something bad and didn't get caught, that was a real blessing!

So when it came to reading this verse as a young Christian I had no clue what Paul meant when he said in Eph 1:3 that God had *"blessed us with every spiritual blessing in the heavenly places in Christ."*

What were these spiritual blessings? What did that verse mean? Now I know, and I get to live from that place of being blessed by God every single day.

Basically, to break it down into modern-day English, the word "blessing" means 'spoken blessing, generosity or benefits'. So God has spoken over us every good thing He could think of to speak, and in doing so sent His word to accomplish the release of those good things into our lives (Isa 55:11). He sent that spoken blessing to deliver into our lives all His generosity, and the uncountable benefits of knowing Him.

This whole chapter in Ephesians outlines some of those blessings that have been given to you...

- You were chosen before the foundation of the world (v.4).

- You have been made holy and blameless (v.4).

- You have received, and been established in, His Love (v.4).

- God adopted you into His family and you became His own dearly loved child (v.5).

- You are accepted in the Beloved (v.6).

- You have redemption through His Blood (v.7).

- Your sins are forgiven (v.7).

- All the riches of His Grace abound to You (v.7-8).

- He has made known to you, and will continue to make known to You, the mystery of His will (v.9).

- You have obtained an eternal inheritance (v.11).

- You have heard the Word of Truth (v.13).

- You are sealed with the Holy Spirit of Promise (v.13).

- You know the hope of His calling (v.18).

- You know the exceeding greatness of His power (v.19-20).

And these are just the blessings this chapter tells you about. On top of that you have been set free from sin's dominion, made whole, and become joint-heirs of the Kingdom of God with Jesus. You have received power from the Holy Spirit, been filled with the fullness of the Godhead, healed by the power of Christ's work on the cross, all your needs have been provided for, and loads more. These blessings of God have been sent by the Word of God from the spiritual realm and have been released into your earthly life.

Wow! That's a praise party waiting to happen right there! Why don't you take a moment and just pick one of the blessings given you in Christ that are listed above, and thank God for it. But also ask Him to tell you what that means for you personally, and how He wants it to be worked out in your life. As you do you'll receive revelation that will add extra depth and richness to that blessing in your life, causing it to become increased until it is a good measure, pressed down, shaken together and running over, poured into your lap (Luke 6:38-40).

JOURNAL PAGES...

YOU ARE A PEARL OF GREAT PRICE

DAY FOURTEEN

"... the kingdom of heaven is like a merchant looking for fine pearls. When he found one of great value, he went away and sold everything he had and bought it." (Matt 13:45-46).

I used to think that this passage of Scripture was telling me that I had to give up everything to enter the Kingdom of Heaven and obtain Christ. I thought it was telling me that my giving up everything, would be how I would get a relationship with Christ; as if my works could ever be enough to obtain Christ for me, bring Him into my life, and make Him mine.

But later, as I realised that my works could not bring salvation and relationship with Christ, I began to view it differently, and read it as a reminder of how precious the Kingdom of God was, and of the need to treasure Christ and all that He'd done for me, and because of that I could gladly give myself, and all I had and was, to Him.

Still later God challenged me to view this differently again. What if, in fact, I was a pearl of great price that all of Heaven thought was worth obtaining? What if Christ had given all He had for me because He wanted me in His life so much? He looked beyond my fragility, brokenness, and sin, and saw something of inestimable worth and value, and He gave everything so that I might be His. I saw a picture of His grace, His self-sacrifice, His love and desire, and of my eternal worth and value, and it humbled me. To think that God viewed me like that, and gave me that much value, filled me with a sense of humility and gratitude. I now think this is more in line with Jesus' original intent in saying this. He was telling us how much value all of Heaven places on our lives.

We move through phases in our growth, where as we receive more revelation we view things differently. That's how it should be; we know in part, and therefore must be open to more revelation, more light coming into our life. Sometimes it's good to go back to Scriptural truths and ponder on them again, to allow different things to be shown to us, to see them from new perspectives.

It's also not unusual for God to use the same Scripture to speak different things to us at different times. His ability to do this is something that fills me with wonder! I pray that today this passage of Scripture becomes a place of fresh revelation for you and blesses you in new ways as you read it.

JOURNAL PAGES...

YOU ARE HIGHLY FAVOURED

DAY FIFTEEN

In my life as I grew up, 'being favoured' wasn't something I knew, unless it was being singled-out for something bad to happen to. Being favoured in a good way happened to other people, but not to me, not to our family. Our family had 9 kids, we were poor, wore second-hand clothes, second-hand shoes, we were dirty and unkempt and therefore were ostracised and picked on at school. We were the kids no-one wanted on their team or in their group of friends. School was hard, but home was harder; and the word 'favoured' had different, even more horrible, connotations in my home, where abuse of varying kinds was a common occurrence.

So for me, when I first came to know Christ, I thought that the Scriptures about knowing the good kind of "favour" from the Lord applied to others, but not to me... until I discovered that God actually really did love me. Along the way I also discovered what the word favoured meant Scripturally; it means – *to be shown kindness to, and to be cherished; demonstrated delight and approval; to show grace toward.*

Little by little the fact that I was favoured by God began to sink in. God wanted to show me His kindness and for me to know that I was cherished. He wanted to demonstrate His delight in me and His approval of me.

He wants you to know that you, too, are favoured – by the Trinity and by all of Heaven. You are loved, cherished, delighted in and shown grace. Yet look online at some Christian articles and they tell you another story – a story about how you can earn the favour of God, and grow in favour with God. One article I read set out ten things you can do to find favour with God. According to this, and other articles that I read, if you do certain things you will find the favour of God extended toward you, and that will be evidenced in things like – you'll get promoted, you'll find things going in your favour, you'll get praised, platforms will open up to you, etc.

Performance-based acceptance and favour is not what God has in mind for His relationship with you. You are favoured by God because He is love, goodness, and kindness, and He wants to reveal His love – to show you that He delights in you and cherishes you, His loved one.

In Luke 2:52, when it talks about Jesus growing in favour with God and man, I don't believe it's talking about Jesus proving Himself so that God and men would be happy with Him; because, as we know, mankind certainly didn't show acceptance of Him and they put Him to a horrible death. It's about Jesus growing in the ability to walk out His life from a place of knowing that He was delighted in, cherished, shown grace, and loved, that He lived in the favour of God and was growing inside it. The more He did this the more the evidence of that favour grew around His life and was seen and felt by mankind, but it was never based on Him having to perform well in order to grow in favour.

Like Jesus, You are delighted in, cherished, and loved; the favour of God is extended toward you and it will be with you forever. As you allow God to show you how favoured and loved by Him you are, the evidence of that will be seen in your life. You will walk with greater confidence and boldness, showing to all that you know you are a much loved child of the King and the provisions of the Kingdom are made available to you.

JOURNAL PAGES...

YOU ARE LOVED, THE APPLE OF HIS EYE

DAY SIXTEEN

David prays in Psalm 17:8, *"Keep me as the apple of your eye; hide me in the shadow of your wings."*

Have you ever wondered what the term 'the apple of your eye' means? It comes from a Hebrew expression that means "little man of the eye", which refers to the tiny reflection of yourself that you can see when you look into another person's eyes.

For David to ask God to keep him as the apple of his eye means that David was talking about being able to be up close and personal enough to see the reflection of himself there in God's eye, that God would be gazing upon David, watching him closely.

I believe that somehow, by the grace of God, David had seen beyond the covenant he lived under into the New Covenant reality of sonship that mankind could share with God, and also into the face-to-face relationship shared by the Trinity and spoken about in John 1. This is where John says that the Word was with God – that phrase literally means that Jesus (the Word) was face to face with God the Father.

All through this Psalm we see David's trust in God's love and favour. David knew that because of that relationship God would listen to his prayer, that he could ask for protection and that God would answer his prayer (v. 6). David was confident that God would show him the wonders of His great love and that he would be vindicated before his enemies (v.15).

Just like David, we can be this confident in God and His love for us. We can be assured that God hears us when we pray and will answer our prayers. We can know that we, too, are the apple of His eye, that His gaze is on us, that He is watching over us and that He will protect us from the enemy's plans to destroy us.

And while that doesn't mean that nothing bad will happen in life, it does mean that because we are cherished in His sight that He will lead us through all things and help us. He will give us strength and encouragement, strategic insight and help from heaven so that we can stand and emerge as overcomers.

JOURNAL PAGES...

YOU SPOKE TO YOURSELF AS SOMEONE WHO IS LOVED BY GOD

DAY SEVENTEEN

You are the person you listen to most in life – not your parents, not your peers, not your teachers or boss, not even God, but yourself! If that's true then what are you saying to yourself? What's the soundtrack that is constantly running in your mind, and does it agree with what God says about you?

Most of us live with an internal sound-track playing in our life, a running commentary on our interactions with life, that we've got used to and now it's just part of our everyday life. It's the thoughts we have about ourselves, our actions, our appearance, and our feelings; all day every day.

If you're awake, your self-talk soundtrack is running.

However most of us never stop and think about what our self-talk soundtrack is saying to us; most of the time we simply listen to it without evaluating whether it's true, useful, or helpful.

If the conversations in our head are negative then the chances are high that we will not be living our life to our full potential, and those internal conversations are probably not in agreement with how God views us, or the kind of life that He has for us to live.

That negative, critical, poor, image you have of yourself, it is just that – an image; it is not who you truly are. It's a mix of heaps of different influences, things such as...

- What your parents taught you – both intentionally and the kind of things you heard them say around the house.

- The social norms you absorbed growing up.

- What your friends think and talk about.

- The kind of education you had.

- The kind of media you consume.

- Your own unique view of the world.

- The lies of the enemy of your soul, the devil, the one whose sole aim is to steal, kill and destroy.

- The voice of God speaking life and imparting life and strength in all that He speaks.

Your self-talk soundtrack is a remix of all those influences, filtered through your own life experiences and your thinking patterns. **Most of us are more attuned to the negative aspects of our thought life rather than being attuned to God. That ability to listen to and come into agreement with God in our internal dialogue usually takes time and effort to develop. It takes bringing our thoughts into submission to both our heart and mind, as the steward of our life, and to Christ in us. It takes us being intentional about what we listen to.**

We all know the kind of music we like to listen to and many of us make soundtracks with our favourite songs on that we play often. These songs are often ones that have an emotional connection to different times in our life – specific points where that song encapsulated something about how we felt about the moment, ourselves in the moment, good memories, sad memories etc. What if...from today we choose a new internal soundtrack to listen to? How about we build a new internal dialogue, based on agreeing with how God sees us. What would change in our life as a result? I wonder...

JOURNAL PAGES...

WE LIVED FROM DELIGHT

DAY EIGHTEEN

We read clearly in Scripture that God loves us, He delights in us, and He dances and sings over us. What if we lived from the knowledge of that daily? How different would our day, our life, be? What if we settled forever the questions of whether God actually likes us, is happy with us and our progress, whether He secretly wishes we were more like someone else, etc? What if we lived from the delight that the Trinity have when they look at us? In relation to your life, what change would that make?

Worrying about whether God loves us, likes us, or is happy with us uses emotional and mental energy that could much better be used in living from the place of knowing that God delights in us, accepts and loves us.

God doesn't mean for us to live our lives wondering whether we're in or we're out, accepted or rejected, liked or disliked, smiled on or frowned upon. Yet so many Christians live in that state of uncertainty. They think that the Trinity sit in a constant state of judgement, watching and assessing every single thing they do to see if they are good enough. Yet in John 8:15 Jesus said of Himself that He came to judge no-one... *"You judge according to the flesh, I judge no one. Yet even if I do (choose to) judge, my judgment is true, for it is not I alone that judge, but I and he who sent me."*

Jesus said that He judged no-one. The purpose of His coming was not to judge the world, but that through Him the world might be saved. He came to offer salvation to those who choose to receive Him and believe His goodness. But as He said in the Scripture, even if He did choose to judge, His judgements are just and true. Jesus, being God knows the heart of God for mankind, and He also knows the hearts of men and their motivations, so He can see what man cannot see. He judges from the perspective of being the one who filters all His seeing and knowing through love and understanding.

Interestingly Jesus said this about the Father in John 5:22- 24, *"For the Father judges no one, but has given all judgment to the Son, that all may honour the Son, just as they honour the Father. Whoever does not honour the Son does not honour the Father who sent him. Truly, truly, I say to you, whoever hears my word and believes him who sent me has eternal life. He does not come into judgment, but has passed from death to life."*

So neither Jesus or the Father sit and judge us. So then what was the judgement they made? They judged the separation and sin issues and made the judgement call that they would do something about it – and they did! Now you and I get to live from the place of restoration and delight that the Trinity's judgement of separation and sin brought us into. Here's some verses to ponder on. Allow the truth of them to sink in and change forever the way you see your relationship with the Trinity, as one who is loved, accepted, delighted in, and celebrated.

"For the Lord takes pleasure in His people; He will beautify the afflicted ones with salvation." Psa 149:4.

"The Lord your God is in your midst, a mighty one who will save; he will rejoice over you with gladness; he will quiet you by his love; he will exult over you with loud singing." Zeph 3:17.

"He brought me out into a broad place; he rescued me, because he delighted in me." Psa 18:19.

"You shall be a crown of beauty in the hand of the Lord, and a royal diadem in the hand of your God. You shall no more be termed Forsaken, and your land shall no more be termed Desolate, but you shall be called My Delight Is in Her, and your land Married; for the Lord delights in you, and your land shall be married. For as a young man marries a young woman, so shall your sons marry you, and as the bridegroom rejoices over the bride, so shall your God rejoice over you." Isa 62:3-5.

"But the Lord takes pleasure in those who fear him, in those who hope in his steadfast love." Psa 147:11.

"The steps of a man are established by the Lord, when he delights in his way." Psa 37:23.

The Lord says that you are not forsaken, not an orphan, not unloved or unwanted, not disapproved of or looked down on. Instead this is the place you get to live from – the place of being loved, delighted in, and celebrated! Believe it, embrace it and live from that delight.

JOURNAL PAGES...

YOU ARE THE HABITATION OF GOD

DAY NINETEEN

Years ago there was a song that Bette Midler made popular. It encapsulated the belief of many people in the world today – that God is a distant bystander watching us from far away. I used to believe that about God, that He had no real interest in my life except to check-in every once in a while to see if I was still being bad. Hearing the Good News changed all that. God was not distant; in fact, He cared so much that He came and did something about the separation issue.

It fascinates me, this thought that Christ now dwells in me, that the Trinity would much rather be so up close and personal that they choose to make their home in us instead of some musty, dusty building or temple made by human hands. How fitting that the temple they dwell in is not a temple designed and created by man, but one originally designed and created by themselves. Who better than them to know what sort of dwelling place best suits them, and who better to build it! We know that Scripture tells us that we are the temple of the Holy Spirit and that Christ dwells in us, and because Jesus and the Father are one that means the Trinity – all of them – have made their home in us.

In 2 Cor 13:5 the apostle Paul asks the Corinthian believers a question: *"Or do you not realize (this) about yourselves that Jesus Christ is in you?"*

And in 1 Cor 3:16 we read, *"Do you not know that you are God's temple and that God's Spirit dwells in you?"*

The wonderful truth is this – in what Christ has done, God is not a distant God, and we do not worship Him from afar. You and I are His children and we bear His image. He made us holy and righteous through the work of Christ on the cross. He gave us eternal life and resurrection power flows in our lives through the power of the empty tomb (Rom. 6:1-6), and He now lives in us.

We are no longer flawed image-bearers under the dominion of sin which caused separation; we are new creations, image-bearers who have been given even more wonderful benefits than Adam and Eve knew. We are, wonder of wonders, made into a fitting place for God to dwell, we are the temple and dwelling place of God! And, that's not pride saying that, it's truth!

Religion will try and tell you and I that we must do a heap of work to make ourselves a fit place for God to dwell, that we must clean up this and that, and stop doing such and such. But the truth is when God dwells in you and you are made a new creation, much of that stuff that religion says we must work hard to rid ourselves of simply falls away because it's no longer who we are, and it happens as we grow in our understanding of our new identity. Our mind is renewed and we are transformed. Instead of being sin-focused, trying to resist and stop certain things, we become focused on living from our righteousness and holiness, letting those newly engrafted things within us grow, mature and bear their fruit.

We are growing in the ability to think as Christ thought, say what Christ said, and do what Christ did. It's a growth process that takes place and comes into maturity over time. (See John 15:1-8; 17:26; Rom 8:10,29; Eph 3:19; 5:1; 2 Pet 1:4; 1 John 2:6,24,27,28; 3:24; 4:16.)

What does it mean that we're now the dwelling place of God? How does that outwork in our lives? Simply put it is to know that we are loved, to become a living manifestation of love, and to show others God that loves them. That can be done in a multitude of ways. We get to show others what it looks like to be loved by the Trinity, indwelt by them, set free by them, provisioned by them, and gifted with eternal resources that bring freedom and life. How mind-blowingly awesome is that!

JOURNAL PAGES...

GOD HAS MORE GOOD IN STORE FOR YOU THAN YOU CAN EVER IMAGINE

DAY TWENTY

I love reading Ephesians; it's so full of God's rich goodness toward us in Christ. Here we find Paul, who had been through so much, and would yet go through even more because of his love for Christ – being persecuted, beaten, shipwrecked, jailed, and hunted down by both religious and civic leaders. Yet here in the midst of all that we find this chapter, Ephesians 3, where Paul prays that we will be strengthened with power in our inner being through the Holy Spirit, rooted and established in God's love, able to grasp how deep and wide the love of God is for us, and that we will know experientially that love, so that we may be filled with the fullness of God! Wow!

And, as if that is not enough goodness for us to handle, he says this to us, *"Now to him who is able to do immeasurably more than all we ask or imagine, according to his power that is at work within us..."* (Eph 3:20)

We're all familiar with the saying, "But wait, there's more", and usually when we hear it we cringe because we know some salesman is trying to sweeten the deal to make us buy something. But here, when Paul in effect says that very thing, he is saying, "Yeah God's good, but He's even better than you think. He loves you more than you know and wants to do more in, and through, your life than you could ever imagine. Whatever you can dream – it's not big enough; He can do more! Whatever your problem – He's not worried about it; He is well able to do above and beyond what's needed to bring good out of it and turn it to bless you."

And here we are today, in the midst of global turmoil, facing many sorts of problems. But even here in the midst of riots, racial tensions, a global recession, jobs being lost, travel restrictions, businesses closing, and people dying, God can, and will, do immeasurably more good than we can hope or dream. He will make this work for good. Watch, you'll see. Stay in faith, stay believing that your heavenly Father is good – because He is!

Look for His goodness in the middle of it all – the sudden revelation from Scripture, the worship song that blesses, the unexpected gift from someone, increased sales of your inventory, kindnesses you weren't expecting, neighbours you've never talked to before becoming friends, new jobs etc. His goodness and His 'immeasurably more' comes in so many unexpected ways. Can I suggest that you take some time today to recall His goodness in your life in the past, and thank Him for what He's about to do as He unleashes immeasurably more into your life; I will be.

JOURNAL PAGES...

GOD REALLY DOES HAVE A STRATEGY FOR YOUR PRESENT CIRCUMSTANCES

DAY TWENTY ONE

One of the things I've loved reading over the years in Scripture is how, when Israel came into difficult circumstances or battles, they enquired of the Lord and He gave them a strategy for that situation and I found it interesting that the strategy that God gave them was different for each situation they found themselves in.

Today's challenge to us is – do we ask Him to show us His strategy for our current situation, or do we just assume He will use be the same strategy as in the last situation we faced. Or maybe we try and come up with our own strategy and battle through in our own strength?

As He did in Scripture with Israel, God does have a strategy for our circumstances, and He will show us if we ask Him. God's ways are often very different from ours. He knows what is happening behind the scenes and when we flow with His strategy our battle is won or the situation is resolved. His strategy may sound strange, it may ask things of us that we don't understand, it may need a mind-shift to take place in us, it may challenge how much we really trust Him, and more. Each challenge is different and we can't apply the same strategy to every situation we find ourselves in.

A lot of the time we just want our challenges gone and our situations fixed, and fixed fast. We want to get back to life as normal as quickly as possible, to feel undisturbed again. Does this sound familiar to you? We want our situations fixed. Sometimes because they legitimately need a solution – an injustice has been done, or we need a new job, bills need to be paid, etc. Other times we want them changed or resolved because we feel uncomfortable or threatened, our identity feels challenged, our reputation is suffering, we, or our family, are suffering and it feels like some of our perceived rights have been challenged or removed.

God's strategies for our situations usually work in two areas simultaneously; on the situation to bring resolution, and on us – to change us and help us grow. God's strategies are never just about caring for our circumstances; they are also about caring for us, forming Christ in us, and changing us from one degree of glory to another. He has grand plans within His strategy for each situation, and they are way beyond simply fixing a problem.

There are times when our battles and challenges need something in us to change in order for us to rise above them as different people from the people who went into that battle. It's the person who changes that becomes the overcomer, because sometimes we just cannot fully win a battle being who we currently are. We see that in David's life in Scripture – David started out as a shepherd boy, but his hardships and battles, while real and needing solutions, were also preparing in him something more; he was growing into his ability to stand one day as King.

Whatever you are currently facing – don't just ask God to sovereignly fix it, talk to Him and ask Him about His strategy for it. That way the problem will not only find a resolution but you will grow immeasurably because you worked with God in it.

JOURNAL PAGES...

IN GOD, ALL THINGS REALLY DO WORK TOGETHER FOR GOOD

DAY TWENTY TWO

For many years this verse in Rom 8:28 was one I quoted, and to be honest, only semi-believed. *"And we know that all things work together for good to those who love God, to those who are called according to His purpose."*

I saw some of the stuff in my life, especially the horrific stuff that happened to me as a child, and I wondered how God could redeem that and make it work for good. Even after I became a Christian there was some stuff that happened in my life that I wondered how God could ever work anything good from. I suspect we all have situations we can think of like that.

Yet in it all I had to choose to look at God's record of trustworthiness in my life, His love for me, and the ways He had come through and provided on so many occasions. I had to choose to believe that this Scripture was true; to believe that God wasn't lying to me. Then I began to ask God to give me eyes to see the ways that He worked things for good, and I began to see them. I came to realise that God had taken the abuse I suffered as a child and had worked into me an understanding of suffering so that I could sit with others who suffered. He had worked in me a desire to see justice done in the world. He had worked in me a precious release of creativity and imagination that was amazing. He had worked in me the hope for a better tomorrow. Let me tell you how He did that last one.

Imagine this – Here I was a young girl (under 10) sitting on my doorstep escaping from my childhood abuse into a day-dream world of visiting Disneyland. Why Disneyland? Because our TV told me it was the happiest place on earth, and it had a place in it called Tomorrowland. Tomorrowland was all about the hope of a better future, made better by advancements in mankind's ability to create things that would improve the life of everyone alive. I longed for a future like that, a better one than my present. That was one of my escapes from the abuse I was suffering.

Little did I know it but the Spirit of God, who is at work drawing us to the Trinity right throughout our lives, was showing me that all was not lost; there was hope. I didn't recognise that it was the work of God at the time, after all I didn't know God then, and I wouldn't for several more years. Even for many years after I became a Christian I still didn't recognise it as God giving me hope. I just thought it was a thing I did to escape and keep sane in a world that was ugly. Then one day when

I was talking to God about that time in my life He showed me how He had planted hope in my heart through that dream of a better tomorrow – through Walt Disney and Disneyland. Not through a Bible verse, not through going to church, not through some seemingly proper and acceptable religious or Christian thing, but through a secular and, some would say, worldly thing. God took something I could relate to and began to do a work of redemption in my life. That's usually how God works, he takes things we can relate to and starts there.

Over the years He has redeemed so much of what happened to me in my childhood and made it work for my good and the good of others. What the enemy meant for evil God took and used to do a work in me, to help make me who I am today.

By the way, I finally got to actually visit Disneyland several years ago, to stand in that place and see in my life the goodness and redemptive power of God, who took a young abused girl and redeemed her life – all of it, and made something beautiful out of even the dark, ugly, parts that the enemy of my soul meant for evil.

Here's The Passion translation of that same verse. *"So we are convinced that every detail of our lives is continually woven together to fit into God's perfect plan of bringing good into our lives, for we are his lovers who have been called to fulfil his designed purpose."*

It's okay if you still struggle to see where God is taking aspects of your life and is working them for your good. It's okay to struggle to believe this verse. That's not where you'll stay, though. God is at work in you and He will prove Himself to you over time. He will keep proving Himself to you until you, too, become convinced that He means to redeem all your life and to bring good into every part of it. Every day He is working, adding to His track record of faithfulness, love and care in your life. Ask Him to open your eyes to see and recognise how things fit together, how it all relates, and thank Him when He does.

(If you need help with undealt with soul wounds please search out someone qualified who can help you. There are many good healing ministries that God has raised up to help minister to people who have emotional wounds that need healing. Some of them are SOZO, Theophostic ministry, Lie-busting, professional counsellors, and more. Your local pastor should be able to put you in touch with someone who can help minister to you.)

JOURNAL PAGES...

OUR DISILLUSIONMENTS IN LIFE ARE DOING AN ESSENTIAL WORK IN US

DAY TWENTY THREE

Disappointments, disillusionment, people wounds, unmet expectations, prejudice being shown against us, etc. – these are all part of life and, for many of us, they are an annoying part of life that we'd love to do away with. We want life to be plain-sailing, easy, with no bumps in the road. But that type of life will never see us grow and develop; it will never be one where, as Scripture says, *"the seed falls into the ground and dies in order to bear fruit"* or where *"we pick up our cross daily and follow Him"* (Luke 9:23).

It's often not until our present life falls apart in some way that we seek anything more. And until it falls apart we will never see what it is that truly sustains us, what it is we are actually relying on. We need these 'falling-apart's, these small 'dying's in our life – they help us die to our false self, our illusions, our ego, and they help us come to grips with, and understand, our true identity in God.

This is the process Scripture talks about in that verse about the seed in John 12:24, *"Truly, truly, I say to you, unless a grain of wheat falls into the earth and dies, it remains alone; but if it dies, it bears much fruit."* While Jesus was talking about His death and resurrection in this verse, we know it can also apply to our lives in big and small ways.

Jesus' death to self during His life, and His death on the cross were sacred entrustments given to Him by the Father so that all mankind would come to benefit forever from how He handled them, and the work that was accomplished through them.

An entrustment is when something is put into the care of a particular person, assigning them a responsibility. A sacred entrustment is one that is connected with God and dedicated to a sacred purpose. Jesus' life, and the way He approached and handled His death, was a sacred entrustment.

I want to suggest today that we reframe the way we see the small dying's in life such as disappointment, disillusionment, unmet expectations etc. – all those things I mentioned above. If these things are doing an essential work in our life – bringing about a necessary dying to ego and to our false self – then they will also, while causing a death to something, bring about new life in us and ultimately bear much fruit. If that is so, then I want to suggest that we view them as sacred entrustments. I want to suggest that if we mean our life to count in this world, we need to learn how to handle these dying's so that we, and the people around us, will benefit from the resurrection life and fruit that comes from our having handled them well.

I love this quote from Richard Rohr, *"We must trust the pain and not get rid of it until we have learned its lessons. The suffering can be seen as a part of the great pattern of how God is transforming all things. If there is one consistent and clear revelation in the Bible it is that the God of Israel is the one who turns death into life (see Isa 26:19; Rom 4:17; 2 Cor 1:9). When we can trust the transformative pattern, and that God is in the suffering, our wounds become sacred wounds. The actual and ordinary life journey becomes itself the godly journey. We trust God to be in all things, even in sin and suffering."*

JOURNAL PAGES...

EVERYTHING HAPPENING AROUND YOU RIGHT NOW WAS HAPPENING FOR YOU, NOT TO YOU

DAY TWENTY FOUR

Sometimes re-framing how we see things can help us approach things from a different perspective. As a survivor of childhood sexual abuse I viewed the world in a certain way. I was convinced that people were out to use and abuse me and that my whole life would be one long battle of trying to protect myself. Life, and the situations in it, was something that happened to me and conspired against me, and I had to try and survive it.

Back then I had no idea that God's plan was to take all that happened in life and make it work for my good. He promises to do so and He does not lie.

"And we know that all things work together for good to those who love God, to those who are the called according to His purpose." Rom 8:28.

Let me explain. That verse doesn't say, or mean, that God causes all the things that happen, or even that He gives permission for them to happen. But if God is for us then His desire is also to make all of life work for us, to make it work for our good. This is true on both a macro and micro level. In all that happens God is there, waiting for us to see that He is for us in that moment, in that situation. Our part is to look for Him there and see what He is doing "for us". Revelation may be waiting in that moment for us, growth may be there for us to embrace, understanding waiting to enlighten us, and wisdom and provision may be there for us to access. The Trinity are there for us along with their power and provision, waiting for us to find them in the midst of it all. And in finding them in the midst of it all we find rest, peace, provision, joy, purpose, and more.

God knows the plans that He has for us (Jer 29:11) and He plans to do us good, and as we see Him for the good Father He is, we know that we will find His will to be good, acceptable and perfect for us.

What if, when we faced a situation, we didn't think, "Why is this happening to me?" What if we thought instead, "What is hidden in this for me?" "How can this work for me?" "What treasures does God have in store for me in this situation?" "Where can I find God inside this situation?"

If we go into our days with this perspective – that things are for us, no matter how negative they may first appear – then every situation we encounter in life is one that works for our good and it becomes one from which we can receive the treasures hidden within it. I know, it may sound like positivity on steroids to some of you because you are so used to feeling, as I did, that life was working against you, but this is truth. God is for us and is working to make all things work together for good. It's a truth that can set us free.

Do I always remember to view life like this? No, sometimes I forget and fall down the proverbial 'rabbit-hole' into a place of frustration, feeling picked on, disillusionment, and anger. Sometimes in my past I've spiralled down into depression and even despair.

Viewing life as happening 'to you' usually leads down that spiral rabbit hole into negativity; it rarely leads to good thoughts.

Think about that for a moment; maybe you can relate to that. Maybe a perspective change is needed for you, as it was for me. Today, test it out. Go into the day choosing that today is going to happen 'for you'. Look for God in the middle of all that happens. He is there somewhere, waiting for you to see Him and the provision He has made in that situation for you. If you do you will find that your attitude and expectations will change, and you'll realise that in God, all things do work together for your good. They work for you, not just happen to you.

JOURNAL PAGES...

THE WAY GOD ANSWERS OUR PRAYERS REALLY IS FOR OUR GOOD

DAY TWENTY FIVE

God is good! That's one of the central messages and realities of Christianity. Yet how much do we trust Him? How much do I trust Him? How much do we believe that He wants to be good to us, that He is a loving Father etc. Hopefully over these chapters I've been able to show you, and you've had a revelation for yourself that He is good.

I don't know if you've struggled with the whole 'answer to prayer' thing over the years, but I have. In the end, for me, it has come down to this – is God trustworthy? Is He actually really faithful? Can I trust that He knows what is best for me and that He is at work in my life – working all things together for good?

Over the years, as you can imagine from my sharing a brief glimpse into my childhood, trust has been an issue for me – trusting God and trusting people – and while people may not always be trustworthy, I've found that God is. But if you've had a background that has taught you not to trust, how can you know that God is trustworthy? There's a couple of way you can know it.

> 1. Scripture tells us that He is trustworthy:

> *"And those that know Your name will put their trust in You: for You, LORD, have not forsaken those that seek You."* Psa 9:10 (in Hebrew your name means your character.)

> *"Trust in the Lord with all your heart and lean not to your own understanding."* Prov 3:5.

> *"Your decrees are trustworthy."* Psa 93:5.

> *"The works of his hands are faithful and just, established forever to be performed with faithfulness."* Psa 111:7-8.

> *"God is faithful, who has called you into fellowship with his Son, Jesus Christ our Lord."* 1 Cor 1:9.

> *"If we are faithless, he remains faithful, for he cannot disown himself."* 2 Tim 2:13.

> *"Let us hold unswervingly to the hope we profess, for he who promised is faithful."* Heb 10:23.
>
> *"It is impossible for God to lie – his character and his oath(word) prevent it."* Heb 6:14-20.
>
> There are heaps more Scriptures that bear this out also; God is trustworthy and faithful, He can be depended on. If we still struggle to believe it then sometimes we have to choose to remember that our feelings aren't always accurate indicators of truth. Truth stands as truth, whether we believe it, feel it, or not. I had to choose to believe that God was trustworthy, and I also came to feel that sense of trusting Him.
>
> 2. Testimonies from others can attest to someone's trustworthiness – the testimonies we read of God's faithfulness in Scripture, and the ones we hear from people we know, can help us in our search for the truth in that area.

But how does that relate to the answers to prayer that we get, or don't seem to get? Sometimes I don't always get what I pray for and, to be honest, I haven't always understood why not, especially when some Scriptures seem so black and white in what they say. Now, I could get tied-up-in-knots over it, and sometimes I have, or I can recognize that the big issue is not faith, it's trust! That's the bigger thing here. I'm going to say that again –

The big issue is not faith, it's trust!

Do we really trust God? Do we want God to answer in a way that will please us or satisfy us, or do we trust that He knows more than we can currently see? Yes, some Scriptures seem to indicate that He will always answer in a positive way, but many other Scriptures show that not every prayer prayed by people who loved Him were answered in a positive way at the time. But God always made things work for the person's good.

I've found in my personal life that my mind, and the enemy of my soul (the devil), want me to think that I mustn't have enough faith, that I don't believe God enough, and that I'm not strong enough in my stance. The devil wants to use the situation to belittle me, and to bring me into feeling condemned and a failure as a Christian. However I can choose a different response instead. I can choose to trust that God knows what is best, that He can see what I can't, and that He is doing a greater work than I can currently understand. That's not denying a need to have faith, to stand on God's word; instead it's a realization that I don't know everything that's at play. I don't necessarily have all the information and I can't see what God can see.

I'm sure Joseph had to discover that in the things he went through – being betrayed by family, falsely accused and thrown into prison, people breaking promises they made to him, etc. Abraham, Sarah, Naomi and Ruth, David (as he ran from Saul and spent years in a cave), John the Baptist, Paul (and many others in Scripture) had some situations in their lives that didn't receive the 'Christian faith stance' answer to their prayers. But through their lives God proved Himself time and time again to be trustworthy, faithful, true, and loving. He will do the same for you. Will your prayers always be answered the way you hope or expect? Probably not always, but as we discovered in the previous chapter, in the midst of all of life God is working for us, not against us.

JOURNAL PAGES...

HE WHO BEGAN A GOOD WORK IN YOU REALLY WILL COMPLETE IT

DAY TWENTY SIX

We are God's children and here are some things that speak of that – He knew us before we were conceived and loved us even then. His creative power fashioned us in our mother's womb, and He redeemed us in Christ. Right from the beginning He has been at work to do good to us, in us, and through us. So much in Scripture bears this out.

This verse in Phil 1:6 shows us that *"...he who began a good work in you will carry it on to completion until the day of Christ Jesus."*

I'm going to look at this verse from a slightly different angle today to make us think a bit deeper. Sometimes we look at our lives and all we see is that we struggle, we make mistakes, make dumb decisions sometimes, hurt others, speak sharply, etc. We see all the things we do wrong and we feel like God must want to give up on us at times, like maybe He regrets His decision to have us as His child. Or we may know in our head that He loves us, but we don't think that He really likes us that much. Sometimes we do something stupid, or we sin, and then something goes wrong soon after and we can mistakenly think that it was God punishing us for our sin.

Instead of believing that God is loving we believe that He is a hard Father who will do whatever it takes to make us grow, do His will, etc. I had a real example of this one day in a conversation I had with a pastor's wife who had broken her leg. I asked her what had happened and she said that God broke her leg. Her reasoning? God had been asking her to spend more time with Him and she hadn't been obedient so, according to her, He caused her to have an accident and broke her leg so that she would spend more time with Him. My mind boggled that someone could believe that of God, yet we have all at some time or another, probably thought that God would do, or allow, bad things to happen to us to produce His good works in our lives. What twisted thinking that is, yet if we're honest we all have twisted thinking about God somewhere in our life.

The discipline of God does not involve beating you up, speaking down to you, shaming you; those are works of the devil disguising himself as God or as religion. The discipline of God is kind, merciful, loving, non-shaming, firm without being harsh or mean, and calls us up to live from our identity in Him, not puts us down and in our place in a negative way. His works are good because He is good, His work in our life will be kind, because He is kind. His work in our life will be patient, not impatient, and His work in our lives will be ongoing – He will not give up on us or turn His back on us. He will love us to life and wholeness, bringing us into the image of Christ.

He is a good Father, not an abusive, hard, unloving one. The work He does in our lives is a good work done in good ways! Can He be firm at times and speak strongly to us? Yes, but that does not mean that harshness is His nature or character, in any way.

Maybe spend some time today pondering on how you view God, because how you view Him will determine how you view everything that happens to you in life. You will never be able to live with true peace of heart and mind, and real trust in God, if you think that He means to do bad things to you to complete His good work in you.

He has started a good work in you and He will bring it to completion using His good nature and character, doing good things *to you*, *in you*, and *through you*.

JOURNAL PAGES...

WE STOPPED SPEAKING THE LANGUAGE OF SEPARATION FROM GOD

DAY TWENTY SEVEN

Language may be one of the most ordinary aspects of our human life; it is certainly also one of the most important and powerful aspects. Our language – what we say – creates realities, shaping our thinking and everything we do.

We can sometimes get into the habit of saying things without stopping to think about what it is we're actually saying. As Christians, we can get into the habit of saying something because we hear others say it, because it's used in preaching, or is even in the songs we sing in our worship times.

Sadly, sometimes, the things we say or sing reflect a false reality and create a sense of separation from God instead of celebrating our oneness with Him. We speak and sing things that say we are still separated from God somehow, and we need to find Him, to be able to connect with Him. We've spent a lot of time so far in this series of devotions establishing the fact that the Trinity love you, are with you, will never leave you or forsake you, and will supply all your needs. That's why I think it's also important that we look at the language we use – personally, and in our churches.

The two main places, apart from Scripture, that a congregation get their theology and beliefs from are the preaching we listen to and the worship songs we sing.

So what are some of the things we say, or sing, that are in reality Scripturally unsound, or even false statements? What are some of the things that could create a feeling of separation? Some of the things I share next may sound like semantics, but what we say is actually really important. Our logical mind may rationalise and say, "Yes, but what I really mean when I say that is ...", but our subconscious doesn't differentiate between true and false; it accepts everything we say or think as being true. And our subconscious drives much of what we do in life – how we react, how we act. So we subconsciously can set up a belief system that says we are somehow still separated from God, and we need to search Him out, find Him, get closer to Him etc.

Sometimes our feelings may make us think that we don't have what God has promised, and that we have to do something in order to get it, but feelings are not always accurate indicators of truth. We don't always have the feelings of closeness, of satisfaction and fullness, and the devil loves to play on that and tell us that our feelings are in fact truth – that we are not close to God or that we need more of God's presence somehow.

Here are some common statements of separation that we use...

- *We need to stir up our hunger for God, or We need to thirst more for God* – Scripture tells us that when we drink of God we will be satisfied and never be thirsty again. We can desire to deepen our relationship, but we are not beggars seeking a handout of daily crumbs of relational bread (John 4:14; Matt 5:6; John 6:35,44,50-71.)

- *We need to be a God chaser* – God is the divine eternal initiator. Jesus is the mediator between the Godhead and mankind. Through Him they drew us (you and me) to themselves, proved their love for us, and made provision for us to know relationship with them. All we have to do is believe. Once you're in relationship, you don't chase, you enjoy and get to know someone at a deeper level! (John 6:29; Rom 10:9; Acts 16:31.)

- *We need to get close to God* – We are in Christ, made one with the Trinity. You can't get any closer than being 'one' with. We are children of God, not orphans. We can deepen the relationship, but being intimate and brought into Christ is our state of being (1 Cor 6:17; 1 Cor 3:16; Eph 1:5.)

- *Holy Spirit come, we need You to come* – Holy Spirit is not standing outside the building, or outside our lives, waiting to be invited into our services or our daily interactions. The Spirit of God is with us always, dwells within us, has never left us, and never will. (1 Cor 3:16; 2 Tim 1:14; Rom 8:11.) We can ask Holy Spirit to come for specific purposes – come and fill us afresh, come and reveal Yourself to us, but we must never think Holy Spirit is far away or needs a special invitation to come.

- *We want more of you Lord* – Scripture tells us that we have the fullness of the Trinity dwelling within us and available to us. What more is there that they can give of themselves? (Eph 3:19; John 1:16; Col 2:10.)

- *We're desperate for you* – A nice sentiment to say or sing, but it's the language of separation and shows that we don't actually understand what Christ did. Why would we be desperate for Him when He is right there with us and in us? A drowning man, or a person without hope, is desperate, but we have been rescued and brought into safety and security, and hope Himself lives within us. (John 17:13; Rom 15:13; Jer 29:11; Eph 1:18.)

- *We're lost without You* – This is from the same song as the statement above. We were lost, and now are found. We are no longer lost, or without Him, we are very much found and included. We are not orphans but sons and daughters of God. (Eph 2:8,9; Luke 19:10; Luke 15:4; Matt 28:20.)

- *Rend the heavens and come down* – He already did – Jesus came down and changed everything.

- *We need an open heaven* – Jesus opened the heavens at His death and gave us eternal access to God, and nothing has been able to change that.

How often have you used the language of separation from God, unwittingly building that very thing into your reality? I used to do so all too often until I realised what I was doing. Can I encourage and challenge you to change your confession, come into agreement with what Scripture says, and you will see, and feel, the reality of it manifest in your life. The words you use really are that powerful; they really do create the reality you live from.

JOURNAL PAGES...

YOU HAVE BEEN CREATED TO REIGN IN LIFE

DAY TWENTY EIGHT

What does that even mean – to reign in life? Have you ever wondered? I have.

I believe the first place that we learn to reign in life is over ourselves. I'm sure it would have been much easier for God if He hadn't given us autonomy and free will. He could have made puppets, servants with no mind of their own, automatons, but He didn't; He gave us the right to determine who, and what, we do, and who and what we submit ourselves to. With that came a responsibility – to learn how to use that gift, that freedom, wisely; to reign over, or steward well, the life that God gave us.

Reigning in life, as seen throughout the Bible, has much to do with reigning over ourselves. What are some of the things we need to learn to reign over? Our thought-life, our desires, our ego, pride, the desire for power and position, feeling worthless, our tongue, lust, anxiety, criticism, our sense of being right, condemning others, rejection, etc. We must learn to reign over those things otherwise we will live our lives controlled, or ruled, by these things instead of reigning in life, and any position of influence and power that we hold outwardly will be too easily tainted by our character deficits.

Joseph is a good example of one who reigned in life. Joseph's story is told in Genesis chapters 37-50. In telling his story the Bible says little about how Joseph ruled outwardly over people, or within Egypt, but it does show us a lot about how Joseph ruled over his life – for example he ruled over his feelings of rejection and betrayal, over lust and temptation, and over bitterness when imprisoned. He also ruled over unforgiveness in his dealing with his brothers. We also see many examples in Scripture of people who didn't learn to reign over their own lives, and those people did a lot of damage to themselves and to others.

Will we get it perfect? Will we live lives where we make no mistakes? No, but as we grow in Christlikeness we will make fewer of them.

Do we reign outwardly also? Yes! The devil is not the one called to reign in the earth; that responsibility and privilege was given to mankind. God created us in His image so that we would express Him, and He gave us dominion over everything within the earthly realm. In Christ we are called to reign over some things – like sickness, sin, and the demonic. And we are called to reign over the earth itself through our stewardship of it. In Scripture, and throughout history, we see many examples of people who used well the authority that God gave them to reign over these things, and we can be a part of that group.

God's desire is for us to reign in life, but we don't do it just by our willpower; we do it because God, in His goodness, has supplied all that we need to be able to do so. We grow in our ability to reign by letting the life of Christ, and the work of Holy Spirit, transform our hearts and minds. We do it through activating the gifts of holiness and righteousness that we have received which have transformed our very essence, and we do it as we allow the fruits of the Spirit to form and grow in our lives. We learn to reign as our minds are renewed and our lives become transformed, and we do it in the power given us by Christ who lives within us.

JOURNAL PAGES...

WE LIVED AS THOUGH WE HAVE THE MIND OF CHRIST AND THE WISDOM OF GOD DWELLING IN US

DAY TWENTY NINE

I've been a Christian now for almost 50 years and sometimes I look at my life and shake my head at some of the dumb decisions I still make. I'm not perfect, and I don't claim to be, and I wish the "what if..." statement above applied to my life a lot more than it sometimes does.

In the previous chapter we looked at reigning in life and God has given us a great gift to help us in this – the mind of Christ. The Bible tells us that we have the mind of Christ; we have been given access to the thoughts of Christ, to His wisdom, and it encourages us to access that. (1 Cor 2:16; Phil 2:5; Rom 12:2). Yet my life experience shows me that I don't always access it, or ask for wisdom.

There are times for all of us when we make dumb, or bad, decisions, no matter how long we've been a Christian – because we're human. Our decisions are made up of a whole lot of factors and sometimes we don't have all the information we need, or see clearly, when we make a decision. Sometimes we forget that we can ask for wisdom and that we have access to the mind of Christ. And then, of course, when we realise that later we castigate ourselves for not remembering, and we beat ourselves up mentally and determine that next time we won't be so dumb.

But let's take a moment to look back on our lives. I look back on mine and I see that I am a lot wiser than I used to be, I make a lot more good decisions now than I used to. I am growing in maturity, both in the natural and in Christ. My mind is being renewed and, as a result, my life is being transformed. I am accessing the mind of Christ a whole lot more than I used to, and am even doing it unconsciously at times. What do I mean by 'doing it unconsciously'? I mean the Word, both living (Jesus) and written (Scripture), has over time been engrafted into me, become part of me, and is working itself out in my daily life. I am slowly becoming the values I say I espouse, the things I say I believe; I am manifesting more love, patience, kindness, etc. and I'm getting wiser as I let Christ work in me to change me into His image and likeness. I suspect that it's the same for you.

Do I want to access the mind of Christ and His wisdom more than I currently do? Yes! Can we grow more in allowing the wisdom of God to fill our lives and outwork itself in us and through us? Yes! But don't belittle the growth that you've experienced, the changes that have occurred in you, and the ways that the image of Christ has, and is being, formed in you. You are growing up into maturity and while you may have growth spurts, like kids often do, growing into maturity takes time. Continue to let the mind of Christ be formed in you, continue to ask for wisdom, and give yourself permission to not have to be perfect, but to be still growing.

JOURNAL PAGES...

WE HAVE BECOME PARTAKERS OF THE DIVINE NATURE

DAY THIRTY

"His divine power has given us everything we need for a godly life through our knowledge of him who called us by his own glory and goodness. Through these he has given us his very great and precious promises, so that through them you may become partakers of the divine nature, having escaped the corruption in the world caused by evil desires." 2 Pet 1:3-4.

Wow, God has given us everything we need for a godly life! Not one thing has been held back, not one thing that we need has been denied. He has made full, unlimited, provision for us in Christ because of the relationship we have with Him. He has made us promises that He will not renege on, or fail to honour. He is not a liar, so He will keep His promises; and all those promises are so that we may share, or partake in, a reality that is mind-blowing to us as humans.

He has made us partakers of the divine nature. I used to think that means that God, in the work Christ did, reinstated us and helped us recognise what Genesis says – that we are created in His image, a reflection. But it's more than that. We are not only created in His image; in Christ we are invited to *share* His nature, not just *reflect* it. Here's what the word partake means – *to enter into, have the qualities and attributes of, manifest, be characterised by.*

What are some of the characteristics of God, His attributes that you now manifest as your new nature? We find a list of some of them in what we know as the fruits of the Spirit in Gal 5:22-23, but also in 1 Cor 13, as well as many other places in Scripture.

These are some aspects of your new nature...

You are love, and because of that you are loving.
You are kind.
You are merciful.
You are patient.
You are joy, and because of that you release joy everywhere.
You are good, and because of that you do good.
You are forgiving.
You are faithful.
You are gentle.

You have self-control.
You are not given to envy.
You are honourable, honest and trustworthy.
You are not proud, arrogant or boastful.
You do not walk in dishonour, but in honour.
You are not easily angered, and you keep no record of wrongs.
You protect others.
You persevere.
You are holy and righteous.
You are full of hope because you know the one who holds the future in His care.

There's more that we could list, but these are some of the things you can expect God to work in you as your new nature is established in you.

Now if you're anything like me you'll look at that list and think that you don't always measure up well against it, and maybe you don't yet. I sure don't always react, or act, like that, but I also know that growth, and the producing of fruit, is a process. So I'm continuing to explore my new nature, learning about it and what it has provisioned me with, and the things it enables me to do. I am being established in it as I allow Christ to work in me, forming me, and bringing me to maturity, and I'm sure that's what you're doing, too. All the things on that list above are what you can look forward to seeing established in your life as you grow in Christ. This is part of the good work that God began in you and will bring to completion. This is your future and part of your hope. Look at the list again – this is who you are becoming! Wow!

JOURNAL PAGES...

YOU REALLY CAN DO ALL THINGS THROUGH CHRIST WHO STRENGTHENS YOU

DAY THIRTY ONE

When I was preparing these thought-provokers I felt that I had to include this verse, as it's a favourite verse in the Bible for many people. To quote someone else, "How can you not love this uplifting, soul-stirring, take-on-the-world promise?"

But like a lot of verses it can easily over time become something that we glibly quote, and forget how much we actually unknowingly live it each day. The following are some of the ways we can experience the reality of living this verse in our life on an everyday basis. (This list is by no means exhaustive.)

- *We live it in trials* – When we're in times of trial and we turn to Christ for help, and He strengthens us, we are living this verse. (James 1:2-4).

- *When having done all, we stand* – When we come to the end of our rope and we continue to hold on, to persevere, to stand having done all; we are living this verse. (Eph 6:13).

- *When we choose contentment* – It sounds a weird way of living this verse, doesn't it, but when disappointments, setbacks, and delays keep hammering away at us, trying to draw us into living from bitterness, hurt or entitlement, and we, like Paul, choose to be content (Phil 4:12), when we turn instead to seek first the King and His Kingdom, when we turn to gratitude and thanksgiving, we are living this verse.

- *When we continue to pursue the dream that is taking forever to come to pass in our lives* – Sometimes our dreams take time to come to fruition, and sometimes there are setbacks on the way to realising them, but when we continue to choose patience and perseverance in the face of adverse circumstances we are living this verse.

- *When we hold onto peace in the midst of trouble* – Knowing that it is God through Christ who gives us victory (1 Cor 15:57), keeping that inner stance of not letting the enemy take us into fear and doubt – when we do that, we are living this verse.

- *When things are going well* – Believe it or not we can still live this verse when things are going well. Living in the strength of Christ when things are going well is about realising how blessed you are, being thankful, and resting in Him, not relying on your own strength to get stuff done in life. It's also about the work we do in building up inner resources and strengthening mind-sets and establishing truths so that when the hard times come we have a wealth of Scripture and relationship with God to fall back on, to rest against. When we live in good times like this we are living this verse.

There are so many ways that we can live this verse every day. Why don't you take a moment and think about yesterday; think about how Christ strengthened you – in your inner thought life, in your response to situations, with a Scripture, in a phone call from a friend, or with the sense of His presence. I know that you'll find a whole lot of ways He did so, and a whole lots of things to be thankful for.

JOURNAL PAGES...

THE PEACE OF GOD RULED AND WAS GUARD OVER OUR HEART AND MIND AT ALL TIMES

DAY THIRTY TWO

"Be anxious for nothing, but in everything, by prayer and petition, with thanksgiving, present your requests to God. And the peace of God, which surpasses all understanding, will guard your hearts and your minds in Christ Jesus." Phil 4: 6,7.

What would it look like if we allowed the peace of God to actually rule, if we put aside our need to feel in control and to worry, and surrendered to Christ within our heart in this area? How would we move through our days? Is it even possible to do this?

When the peace of God rules it's not about going into denial of circumstances or some make-believe land where nothing is wrong, or will ever go wrong. Scripture is clear that in this world we will face trouble (John 16:33). But it's also clear that when we're God's kids the fruit of peace should be growing and manifesting in our lives until it gets to the place of being the guard of our heart and ruling our heart and minds. Scripture says that in so many verses (see the list below.)

So why do we allow our mind to get filled up with worries and rehearse various possible play-outs and outcomes of situations over and over in our minds, instead of recognizing that it is a form of worry, manifesting in 'what-if' scenarios?

Part of the answer is that we've likely developed a habit of worry. There's a difference between 'being a worrier' and having developed a 'habit of worrying'. 'Being a worrier' means that that's an integral part of who we are – it's coming into agreement with a false identity. Knowing that worry is a habit pattern shifts everything, because habits can be changed. We change habits by repenting – changing our mind, seeing from a different perspective, God's perspective, and then outworking our changed mind into new habit patterns of behaviour.

We have the Spirit of God working in us and with us, giving the grace we need to change, so while it may take some work to establish a new habit pattern, it probably won't take as much work as we think, because of that help. Spend some time today imagining what it would look like if the peace of God ruled and was guard over your heart and mind at all times...

Verses to check out 2 Thess 3:16; Col 3:15; John 14:27; Psa 29:11; Gal 5:22; Phil 4:6-7; 1 Pet 3:11; 1 Pet 5:7; James 3:18; Phil 4:7; Rom 12:17-21; Rom 14:19; Psa 34:14; Isa 9:6.

JOURNAL PAGES...

GOD'S PLAN IS FOR THE RESTORATION OF ALL THINGS

DAY THIRTY THREE

Imagine the world as a better place than it is at the moment. Imagine it as one where the people help each other, are kind and generous, where crime rates drop drastically, animals are cared for and looked after well, where the oceans don't have floating islands of plastic, where governments work for the good of those they govern, and where mankind feels hope.

To some that may sound like idealism, a pipe-dream, a fantasy, and something that could never happen. Sadly, as Christians we are often too ready to condemn the world to a Godless future, to let them destroy themselves, with many Christians believing that we will escape and go somewhere else and leave them to it. Boy, have we ever missed God's heart and intention.

The Hebrews have always understood that God's plans are for the *restoration* of all things, not the *desertion* of all things (Acts 3:21). They believe in that so much that they still pray for it three times each day in their prayer, "Aleinu" (It is incumbent on us). Their belief is that God's plan of redemption in the Messiah will not only save us from eternal separation from God, it will also restore the damage that was caused by sin.

In the beginning God made everything and He said it was "very good" (Gen 1:31). Sure, sin brought destruction into the world, but God's plan of redemption in Christ has saved us from sin and its destruction; it also has bought redemption for all the damage done by sin and Satan. God's plan is that this restoration happens on both a personal and a global level, in personal lives and in the world we live in, in societies and in nature.

The restoration of all things is a central message of Christianity and indeed all the Bible. It's the core of the gospel and it's part of the call of God on our lives – to work with Him as His ambassadors, sons and daughters, and those assigned to steward and care for the earth, to see that work of restoration take place. Some of the things God wants to see restored are – all of mankind restored to relationship with Him, hearts of families restored and turned to each other, the Kingdom of Israel restored to relationship with Him through Christ, natural creation restored, people restored to fullness of health, for people to walk in wholeness, righteousness etc, and, as if that doesn't encompass enough, He says that He wants to restore "all things".

So if God wants to restore all things to Himself, including the earth, then should we as Christians be dreaming of escaping and leaving the earth to chaos, destruction and disorder? If not, then this is where our dreaming with God comes into play.

What's your part in seeing all things restored to God? What's my part? Dare to dream, dare to look around and see what needs restoring, and dare to ask what you can do to work with Him to see it restored. And then, step out and do your part in seeing the restoration of all things manifested and established.

JOURNAL PAGES...

YOU ARE ANOINTED AND WALK IN RESSURECTION POWER

DAY THIRTY FOUR

I used to feel that God couldn't use me as much as some other people – in my eyes they were more skilled, had greater gifts etc.

I had come from a family that believed we could never really amount to anything; I was told that over and over in varying ways. I had people tell me I couldn't do what I felt God had called me to do, that I didn't have what it takes (whatever that means), and I was told that my gender disqualified me from that call. My mind, my internal beliefs about myself and my place in the world, along with other people's beliefs and expectations, all seemed to conspire to create the perfect scenario for me to be an epic failure in life and ministry, someone who would let God down and only ever be a huge disappointment to Him.

I knew what the Bible said – that I was anointed by God and filled with the power of the Holy Spirit – but, in reality, part of me didn't believe it; not really. It took a long time for me to trust that God wasn't a liar, that when He said He had anointed me He meant it, and it was true. Little by little I began to believe that maybe I could move in the anointing of God – in this area or that area. Little by little I took risks, stepped out and trusted that God would do His part, and I saw Him do just that. People began to be touched, ministered to, they began to tell me that the prophecies I gave were accurate and came to pass. People got set free and healed of both emotional and physical things.

Many of you have been, or are, on a journey of coming to believe that you are anointed and filled with the power of God. You might be comfortable in stepping out in some areas but not in others. I have areas where I'm comfortable stepping out and others where I wonder where the anointing is hiding, because I can't seem to find it. I think most people are like that; we're growing and we've grown in some areas faster than in others. And that's okay, as long as we keep growing.

Can I encourage you today, keep stretching yourself, stepping out in faith, taking what you might consider to be a risk. That's where God meets us, in that moment when we step out of the boat, so to speak, when we lay hands on the sick, when we open our mouth and believe that He will fill it. There is a world of people, both outside and within the church, that are waiting on the power and love of God to move through your life; people that you will meet and interact with, that I may not.

Let's stop believing the devil's lies – the ones he tells us now, and the ones we've believed for years. Let's believe God instead, come into agreement with Him, and use the anointing and power He has filled us with to make a difference and release heaven into earth. Yes, there will always be others whose gifts may be more developed than ours, they may seem bolder than we are, or maybe they've just learnt to step out and take risks. Or, maybe they too struggle with the same doubts, but they step out anyway.

Here's some verses you can check out about being anointed by God and filled with His power – 1 John 2:20, 27; 2 Cor 1:21; Isa 61:1; Acts 1:8; 2 Tim 1:7.

JOURNAL PAGES...

TODAY IS A NEW DAY FILLED WITH POSSIBILITIES, HOPE, GRACE AND PROVISION

DAY THIRTY FIVE

Have you ever felt a conflict between dreams of things you'd love to accomplish, and following God's will? I have, I struggled with this for years.

I somehow thought that I had to find out what God's perfect will for me was and only do the things that He commanded me to do. I thought that any dreams I had were nice ideas but probably just my nice ideas and dreams; that they couldn't be from God, and that He couldn't mean me to follow them, because He hadn't told me that He wanted me to do them. So I had dreams that I shelved for years, that slowly withered within me as I sought to walk the tightrope of God's perfect will for my life.

I waited for God to give me orders and did those things that I believed God had assigned for me to do. I saw fruit from them, too, but there was still a problem. I kept dreaming new ideas and seeing new possibilities of things that could be done to release the Kingdom of Heaven into earth. The problem – when I dreamed those dreams, I didn't hear God specifically then tell me to go ahead and do them, to see them become fulfilled, so they languished and slowly died.

Somehow, without realising it, I had slipped into thinking that God was a controlling, micro-managing God who demanded obedience to His will and who didn't want us to have desires and dreams of our own. I didn't realise at the time that I needed to learn to see God from a different perspective so I could see His will from a different perspective. I didn't see that I had mistakenly thought becoming a Christian meant I would no longer be able to make decisions for myself or that I would no longer truly have a free will, or any choice, when it comes to God's plans for my life. There was a stage I went through where I even asked God what clothes I should wear that day, because I'd picked up the idea from somewhere that God wanted total control over every aspect of my life.

I was waiting for God to either give me orders or to override my sovereignty and free will, and plant His desires in my heart. I also thought I would somehow recognise them as being His desires – probably because they wouldn't be something I'd think of, or necessarily want to do. I was expecting God to micro-manage my life, to dictate to me what I could and couldn't do. I didn't think it through and compare that thought to my knowledge that He is a good Father, not an authoritative, domineering dictator.

Yet the truth is – God gave us free will and two of the aspects of that are the ability to self-determine and self-initiate. He never took that away when we became a Christian. He gave us the ability to dream dreams and see things that need changing, to envisage how we can make the world a better place. Yes, we should talk those dreams through with Him – not because we can't move without His approval but because we know He has wisdom that we don't, and He can see things we can't. His strategic insights and help are much needed in our lives.

When our children are little we encourage them to dream. We tell them that they can be anything, do anything, and we help them take steps towards realising the dreams that they have. Some of their dreams are big and some are small, but we don't laugh at them or belittle them. We don't tell them that they must only pursue our dreams for their life. As they grow we teach them the values they need to live from, we teach them practical things that they need to know in order to become a mature productive adult, rather than keeping them as a child. We give them training to help prepare them, and we point them in the direction that will help develop them in ways beyond what we can, in order that they may fulfil those dreams.

So it is with God. He is not wanting to keep you in a place of not being able to move without His permission. He does not see your dreams as insignificant or worthless. His will for your life is that you find what is good, acceptable, and perfect for you. He wants you to live with that sense of purpose and fulfilment. God's plans are not minutely detailed blueprints or a tightrope you must walk or else you're out of the will of God. He is not a dictator or micro-manager. The plans He has for you are to do you good, to bring you to maturity, to form Christ in you, to provide for you, and more. They are not for you to live your life like a puppet who cannot move without its handler pulling its strings.

Dream dreams, plan adventures, recognise the places in society where you can make a difference, talk things through with the Lord, dream and plan together with Him, asking for His advice, His insight. He is wanting adult children, not babies, and your ability to dream and see your dreams come to fruition is part of being a mature son or daughter. As you do you'll realise that today is full of possibilities, hope, grace, and provision in God to see the dreams you dream together with Him come to pass.

JOURNAL PAGES...

YOU CARRY THE SAME WEIGHT OF GLORY THAT JESUS DOES

DAY THIRTY SIX

It's funny how our minds work, isn't it! When I used to think about Jesus and the glory He carried, I imagined Him shining like the sun, unable to be looked on because of His glory and splendour. I hoped that one day maybe, way off in eternity, I might be glorified like Jesus and carry a little bit of a shine or a glow, too.

Then Jesus began to mess with my thoughts and my theology and show me that my ideas of glory, and being glorified, were incomplete. Yes there would come a day when I would be fully seen in all my glory, without anything masking it, and the light that was in me would fully shine with no impediment to stop it. But what I didn't realise was that He wasn't going to wait until I died to fill me with glory, to glorify me; He had already done it. And in fact, even now, I carry the same weight of glory that Jesus has.

To some people that might sound a bit heretical. It almost did to me too, after all, what God was saying to me went against everything I thought and believed about me still being a horrible sinner. Yes, a horrible sinner saved by grace, but still a sinner, destitute and corrupt. I used to believe that one day, maybe, I'd enter into heaven having done just enough to be accepted, and that although God may be disappointed with my life overall, He would let me in because of what Jesus did.

And here God was telling me that I carried the same glory Jesus did – mind-blowing! It was so radically different from the ideas I'd picked up along the way in my early Christian years. I wanted chapter and verse. I wanted proof, so He sent me to Scripture, and there it was in plain sight and coming out of the mouth of Jesus Himself.

"I have given them the glory that you gave me, that they may be one as we are one" – John 17:22.

So of course after I read that it sent me on a journey to find out what Jesus meant by that. What is the glory that was given Him by God? I discovered that the word glory means *"opinion, dignity, judgement, exalted state, magnificence, pre-eminence, and majesty."* Wow, Jesus gave us all that! Believe me when I say that it took a bit of humbling myself to be able to accept that and come into agreement with it. Everything within me wanted to disagree with Him. That wasn't how I saw myself, and it wasn't what the church generally taught.

Then Paul weighed in and in Rom 8:30 he reinforced what Jesus said. *"And those he predestined, he also called; those he called, he also justified; those he justified, he also glorified."* The word 'glorified' in that verse gives us expanded insight and talks about the work He has already done in us in Christ. The fact that you have been glorified means this...

- You are celebrated.

- You are held in high opinion by the Trinity.

- You are honoured (crowned with honour).

- You have been made glorious.

- You have been clothed with splendour and adorned with lustre (the glow of the glory).

- You have been rendered excellent.

- Your dignity and worth have become manifest and are acknowledged.

The Trinity themselves, and all of Heaven, recognise your glory, value and worth and it is forever settled.

Hold your head up high, not in arrogance, but in acceptance. You have been crowned with honour and while the crown you wear may be invisible to some here on earth at the moment, it is seen and recognised by all that inhabit the spiritual realm. One day your full glory will be visible to all – on earth and in the spiritual realm. Rejoice in your glory and value, accept how God sees you, and how He holds you in high esteem. Know who you are – you are a child of the King, loved and honoured by God, given the same glory that Jesus carries, clothed in honour and splendour. Wear your glory well!

Did you notice that as you read that post your body responded – it straightened up a bit, and you held your head a bit higher. That's because your spirit recognised the truth and responded to it! Don't be afraid to display your glory; it's part of how Christ is seen in the earth. God gets no glory from downcast, defeated looking Christians. Shine, it's what you are meant to do!

JOURNAL PAGES...

STRENGTH SOMETIMES LOOKS DIFFERENT FROM WHAT WE'VE THOUGHT

DAY THIRTY SEVEN

In past chapters we talked about perfectionism, religious expectations, and grace. One of the aspects of grace I've discovered is the grace to not have to be strong in my own strength all the time, the grace to lean back and let Jesus hold me and carry me. I'm learning to let His wrap-around presence infuse me with strength, and I'm learning that strength looks different in different situations.

I used to think that I knew what being strong meant. My life experience, and the wounds I suffered from those experiences, told me that I had to be strong in order to look out for myself, protect myself, and make my own way in the world. To me, being strong meant toughening up, being staunch, determined, tenacious, and more. I had this mental picture of what strength looked like – of my face and eyes filled with determination, feet apart in a boxer's stance, arms raised, fists clenched, taking the knocks that life dished out, and fighting back so that life wouldn't destroy me.

The trouble was, becoming strong or toughening up really meant becoming hard, not letting anyone in, going it alone, keeping my walls and barriers up.

And then I met Jesus and He challenged all my ideas about what being strong was. I found out that the sort of strength I used to know was, in reality, a coping and protection mechanism, not true strength.

Have a think about that for a moment. Is your current idea of what being strong means, in reality, a coping and protection mechanism, instead of true strength? So that begs the question – what is true strength?

I discovered that true strength is having the emotional and mental qualities needed to deal with distressing or difficult situations.

Strength has two aspects to it – one is internal and about character, and the other is physical, and the physical is by far the least important. Strength is mostly related to maturing, forming good character in our life and outworking it.

That internal strength gives you the ability to trust God with your life and let Him and people in, instead of pushing them away. It involves taking risks, trust, and vulnerability. Sometimes strength is the ability to get up and face another day, when you want so badly to just hide away, or worse. Or it's the ability to say "No" to temptation. Strength is sticking to your values when compromise seems expedient. It's saying "Yes" to short term inconvenience for long term gain. It's expressing your feelings instead of bottling them up. It's believing in love when people have hurt you. It's turning to Scripture to be strengthened, and being empowered by the Word. It's moving in power, and it's also sometimes standing in peace in the midst of a storm.

Sometimes the greatest strength we can have is the ability to admit weakness, and to tell God that we need His help, and to let others help us also. Sometimes it shows strength to lay down our strength and let God and others be strong on our behalf.

Maybe you're on that grace journey of learning to trust God and others again after having to always be the strong one. God longs to give you the grace you need for that. He wants to be your strength and to give you strength; He doesn't want you to think that you have to 'go it alone'. You don't have to always be the strong one! Look at some of what Scripture says…

"My grace is sufficient for you, for my power is made perfect in weakness.". 2 Cor 12:9.

"For the Lord your God is the one who goes with you to fight for you against your enemies to give you victory." Deut 20:4.

"My soul is weary with sorrow; strengthen me according to your word." Psa 119:28.

"He gives strength to the weary and increases the power of the weak." Isa 40:29.

"The Lord gives strength to his people; the Lord blesses his people with peace." Psa 29:11.

"Those who hope in the LORD will renew their strength. They will soar on wings like eagles; they will run and not grow weary, they will walk and not be faint." Isa 40:31.

"Finally, be strong in the Lord and in his mighty power." Eph 6:10.

God can be trusted and as you grow in Him and learn that you don't have to 'go-it-alone', you don't have to always be the strong one and that you can let others in, it's there you'll find true friendship and family. It's there you'll find a place of rest.

JOURNAL PAGES...

# what if...

WE LOVED AND ACCEPTED PEOPLE LIKE JESUS DOES

DAY THIRTY EIGHT

The fact that we are all loved by God is the core message of the good news, the gospel. It saddens me that in most of society the church is not known for this being its message.

When I was at my worst the Trinity loved me – not just in theory, but in actuality. They showed, and proved, their love in the most amazing way and they continue to do so. As a result I now know their love as my everyday reality. I know that I am loved, accepted and cherished, and the healing and freedom that has brought into my life is nothing short of miraculous!

I have been forgiven of my sins, set free from the pressure to prove myself, to perform for acceptance, to have to earn others' approval. I have been changed by the love and acceptance of Jesus, Father God, and Holy Spirit. This is the good news we have to share; this is what we get to show the world God is like.

A friend of mine, Paul Ellis, inspired this chapter with an article he wrote in which he said this – *"The good news of God's acceptance will change the world, but first it must change the church... When we see that our heavenly Father accepts us it will transform us from the inhospitable church we are to the accepting church we are called to be."*

What would it be like if we loved and accepted others as Christ has loved and accepted us? (Rom 15:7). What would change in people's lives as they learnt that they are loved and accepted in Him at their very worst, just as we were? And as an added bonus, what would change in the way the church is perceived in society?

Over the last few decades God has been relentless in His efforts to get the church to see how loved and accepted they are by Him. He has been working on our knowing who we are. He wants to be able to show the rest of the world through us, that they are loved, accepted, and can know their worth, and value. He wants them to know that they, too, are created in the image of God, so that they can know their true identity. But for the church to cooperate with God in sharing that good news, we must first know it without a doubt for ourselves.

The Holy Spirit and our new nature itself, want to work with what our eternal spirit instinctively knows – the truth of who we were created to be, the truth we instinctively knew as we were being formed in our mother's womb. We were created to be loved, we were created for greatness, we were created for more than we've settled for. God put that knowing within us; it's why we respond to love, and to God. Our true self is responding to what it instinctively knows we were born for.

We are returning to our eternal state, one reserved for us from the foundations of the earth – that of image-bearers and partakers of the divine nature – and we are becoming those who manifest it. We are throwing off our wrong cultural conditioning, other people's opinions about who we are and who we should be. We are unlearning – being set free from false expectations (others and ours) and lies we've believed. We are discovering, and learning to walk out, our new nature, our new creation reality. We are becoming who we were always meant to be, who we truly are.

When we know this as our reality we will show this; the church will truly show God's love. We will love and accept others as Jesus did, in all their messiness, hurt, and sin. The love we show them will do for them what love did for us when it drew us home to the Father who loves us. We will welcome them in, where they too can discover for themselves that they are loved, accepted, celebrated, and have big things dreamed over them.

Imagine what that would look like; the church being known for its love, its acceptance, its welcome, not for the things it's against. Imagine you and I personally being known for our love, acceptance, and openhearted welcome of people into our lives. How would that change things?

JOURNAL PAGES...

THE TRUTH IS BETTER AND MORE FREEING THAN WE'VE EVER BELIEVED

DAY THIRTY NINE

The good news of what Christ did in His life, death, and resurrection actually is good news – really good news – and it is incredibly freeing! His work freed us from the tyranny of sin's dominion over our lives, freed us from separation from God, delivered us from the weight of religion's demands, and much more.

Over the previous chapters we asked questions that have made us think and evaluate what we really believe and, hopefully, we've given you some Scriptural insight that the Lord has used to bring revelation to you. That revelation is something you can now live from, knowing that it's actually truth.

I want to talk about another aspect of the good news in this chapter. The New Covenant really is a new covenant. As New Covenant recipients, and the inhabitants of it, we need to understand that we are not under the law. In fact we were never under the Mosaic covenant; that was only for the Jews, and even for them it was cancelled over 2000 years ago in Christ's death and resurrection.

"Now, however, Jesus has received a much more excellent ministry, just as the covenant He mediates is better and is founded on better promises.... When He said, "A new covenant," He has made the first obsolete. And anything that is obsolete (out of use, annulled, old and useless) is near to disappearing (will die out, cease to exist, wither away, become extinct)." Heb 8:13.

The Old Covenant has been made obsolete – it no longer has any actual power to dictate to anyone.

As Christians we were crucified in Christ, buried in Him, rose again in Him, and are now seated with Him in heavenly places. We live under the terms of the New Covenant made by Jesus and God. Can we learn from the Old Covenant? Yes we can learn from it, but we are not under it.

We are not bound by those laws and if we choose to adhere to them still, and to the covenant that produced them, we must adhere to all of it otherwise we place ourselves under a curse – the curse of the law. *"For all who rely on the works of the law are under a curse, as it is written: "Cursed is everyone who does not continue to do everything written in the Book of the Law."* Gal 3:10.

We can learn from everything that is written in Scripture. As Paul tells us in 2 Tim 3:16, *"All Scripture is inspired by God and profitable for teaching, for reproof, for correction, for training in righteousness."* However we are not required to adhere to everything recorded there in the Bible. Some things in Scripture were written only to specific people, or specific groups of people, not to us. Part of maturing in Christ is learning to discern what was written to someone else that we can learn from, and what is written to us and to all mankind.

I don't know about you but I'd rather live under the covenant Christ made, the covenant of love, liberty, and grace, in the freedom Christ that died to give me. I'd rather live as a New Covenant recipient, a child of God, made holy in Him, living from my new creation nature.

Yes, with freedom comes responsibility, and it requires that we become mature, able to make good decisions based on both our new nature in Christ and from a place of maturity, not simply from obeying laws. That's understood; but that's part of growing up, that's learning to be wise stewards of the gift He has given us.

"It is for freedom that Christ has set us free. Stand firm, then, and do not let yourselves be burdened again by a yoke of slavery." Gal 5:1.

The good news truly is good news, and the truth is more freeing than we've ever believed! What are we going to do with it? How are we going to live as a result of receiving it? Will we live free, stewarding well the gifts He has given us, or will we retreat again to living under the rules and regulations of religious bondage?

JOURNAL PAGES...

WE KEPT ASKING QUESTIONS OF WHAT WE BELIEVE

DAY FORTY

Doing this series of devotions has been great for me. I've been both delighted and challenged as I've delved into what we believe and why we believe it. As I said earlier in this book, this process has been happening to me for years as God Himself has challenged me time and time again to check out whether the things I believe are truth or not. I've squirmed at times and berated myself when I've discovered things that I believed that were not in fact truth. I've also been delighted, and have celebrated, as revelation truth has set me free or reinforced and further established truths that I already knew.

These "what if" thoughts have come out of my desire to know the truth, to discover what God is really like – not what traditional Christian belief tells me about Him, but what He Himself says and what He reveals about Himself through Christ. It's also been about discovering the New Covenant and what living in that covenant means for our lives. My heart in sharing them with you has been that you too would discover truths that would set you free. I hope you've enjoyed traveling this journey with me, that you've been both delighted and challenged along the way, and that you've discovered new aspects of truth about the covenant you live in with God.

But I'd hate to think the journey would stop here. What if we allowed Jesus to continue to challenge our theology? What if we continued to ask questions, to challenge our perspectives, and be open to new revelation and understanding? What if we were willing to admit that our perspective may not be the only possible one, or that our perspective may be wrong, or it may reveal one aspect of truth but not all of it? What if we were willing to admit that we don't know everything and that we may not yet have all the relevant information? What would that mean for our Christian life?

This book is not the last word in regards to truth. I, like you, are on an ongoing journey of discovery and growth. This is simply what I see and know at this point in my journey, and I am comfortable with the fact that I don't know everything, and that my perspectives may need to change still. That must be the case for all of us. As Scripture says – we see in part as if through a darkened mirror (1Cor 13:9,12). We don't have to pretend we know it all, and we can trust that God will increasingly lead us forward into further revelation of truth.

I don't know about you but I want the freedom that Christ died to give me; it's important to me, just as it is to Him. So I'm going to keep asking questions and letting God ask me them, too.

So that leads us here, to this moment. Will you join me in continuing to ask questions, in allowing God to take you deeper into the beauty and mysteries contained in truth? If your answer is "Yes", then I'd love to invite you to picture the following and join me at this moment, in raising a metaphorical glass full of New Covenant wine, full of the goodness of God and overflowing with joy unspeakable – *"Here's to what-if questions! May they continue to reveal truth to us and set us free. May we not only be unafraid of them, may we welcome them and the freedom they bring into our lives."*

JOURNAL PAGES...

About Lyn Packer

Lyn Packer has many years of experience as a pastor, itinerant minister and prophetic voice. She loves seeing people set free to be all they were created to be and to follow the call of God on their lives. As a speaker and teacher her heart for God and her love for people are very evident, as is her solid understanding of Scripture.

Lyn's prophetic and teaching gifts are expressed through a variety of means, in speaking, writing and art. She regularly mentors and trains emerging prophets and prophetic ministers through both her online mentoring groups and the national training school she facilitates. She oversees the New Zealand Prophetic Network and is a member of the New Zealand Prophetic Council. Lyn is also the founder of Together Network – a support and resourcing network for women in leadership roles in New Zealand. As well as her work within New Zealand, Lyn serves on the Global Board of Patricia King's Women in Ministry Network.

Another aspect of Lyn's life and ministry is that of artist and author. As an artist Lyn's work has appeared in group and solo exhibitions and she runs regular prophetic art workshops. She has written books covering a variety of subject matter – prophecy and revelation, creativity, dance, prayer and two books of prophetic allegories. All these books are available on Lyn and Rob's website as listed on the next page.

Websites and contact information

www.robandlyn.org   email – lyn@robandlyn.org
www.nzpropheticnetwork.com   email – office@nzpropheticnetwork.com
www.togethernetwork.co.nz   email – office@togethernetwork.co.nz

More books by Lyn

Visions, Visitations and the Voice of God   Growing in Prophetic Ministry 1&2
Co-creating with God   Free to Dance
Daughters of Eve   Releasing Heaven into Earth
Eyes to See – Dream & Vision interpretation   Whispers from Heaven 1&2

www.ingramcontent.com/pod-product-compliance
Lightning Source LLC
Chambersburg PA
CBHW081154290426
44108CB00018B/2544